We are all in the soup together

PRaise For Transformation Soup

☆ WRitten iN THE STARS...

"Transformation Soup dances me into the darkness and brings me back into the light. Uplifting, wonderfully honest, poignantly funny, and always healing, reading SARK is like finding a precious friend."
-Donna Eden, author of *Energy Medicine*

"Transformation Soup is a vibrant and beautiful exploration of our power to heal ourselves and those we touch. A celebration of the birthright of healing and grace of creativity. Let SARK touch your heart and she will heal you."
-Rachel Naomi Remen, M.D., author of *Kitchen Table Wisdom*

"SARK's delightfully playful and honest viewpoint always reminds me not to get too serious about this giant learning adventure called life." **-Shakti Gawain**, author of *Creative Visualization*

"Transformation Soup is a delightful way to transform old pain into NEW JOY! SARK has done it again. I love this lady. SARK doesn't even know how very wise she is. Long live SARK!!!"
-Louise Hay, author of *You Can Heal Your Life*

OTHer FABulous BOOKS BY SARK

A CReative Companion

inspiration sandwich

Living Juicy

SARK's Journal & Play! Book

The Magic Cottage Address Book

Succulent Wild Woman

The Bodacious Book of Succulence

Change Your Life Without Getting out of Bed

Transformation SOUP

HEALING for the SPLENDIDLY imperfect BY SARK

A Fireside BOOK
PUBLISHED BY SIMON & SCHUSTER
NEW YORK LONDON SYDNEY SINGAPORE

Fireside
Rockefeller Center
1230 Ave of the Americas
New York, NY
10020

Manufactured and printed in our marvelous United States of America

10 9 8 7 6 5 4 3 2 1

(this is where you see How many printings the book has had)

Jupiter sees All

★ Library of Congress Cataloging-in-publication data is available

ISBN: 0-684-85976-9
CIP: 99-052191

This Little creature belongs to Fireside and is a registered trademark of Simon & Schuster Inc. They are kind to let me draw and color it.

Thanks to:
Trish Todd: an excellent editor!
Marcela Landres: wondrous assistance
Cherylynne Li: Thought-Full Art Direction
Jim Thiel: production extraordinaire
All at Simon & Schuster who help these books SPRM

ABUNDANT THANKS
Andrea Scher
super she-ro for her book production work and design and hands. bless you!
love, SARK

ENDEARING THANKS
we are "wondering women!"
TANYA MADOFF
whose book production work is deeply appreciated and also the chocolate chip cookie! mmm!
love, SARK
thanks Ben!

THANK YOU!
To all who graciously gave quotes and permissions, and to the copy editors ♥

MORE THANKS
Here's to CAMP SARK who magnificently supports me in so many ways, including marketing and production for these books!

Transformation Soup

eggs of content

note: READ AS you WISH, and in no PARTiculAr order! or JUST TAKE A NAP...

In process of HEALING

BOOKS and resources AT THE end of EACH CHApTER

HOLY places

WHAT HEALS?

CREATIVE HEALINGS

HEALING THINGS TO DO & WAYS of BEING

You are your own Healer

WE ARE SUCH TENDER little BEINGS, EACH ON A HEALING JOURNEY.

THERE ARE MANY PATHS AND TYPES of Transportation

Let's TALK ABOUT ALL the things THAT DO and DON'T WORK, WHAT Others HAVE tried, and WHAT WE DREAM of HEALING.

I REALIZE NOW THAT MY WHOLE life HAS BEEN ABOUT HEALING. I BEGAN MY NEW year BY DECLARING it MY YEAR of HEALING. I SAW HOW the BUSINESS and WRITING PARTS of MY Life HAD ECLIPSED MY HEALTH and SANITY, and I resolved to inQuire DeePly into HEALING and let it inQuire into ME.

Also BOOKS and experiences

I USED MANY tools: MAGNIFYING GLASS, telescope, microscope, MY SOUL,

So of course, After I MADE MY BiG Declaration of HEALiNG, THE WORLD opened UP BiG HEALiNG Processes riGHT in Front of Me, and CHances for HeaLinG ABOUNDED!

THE BiG HuGE GianT Declaration of HEALinG

OH, Dear.

let's explore toGether, HoLDinG HanDs, and See WHAT SpLenDiDly imperfect HeALinG is All ABout.

let's explore HOLDinG Hands

I think that HEALinG is CALLinG out to US every DAY. HEALinG opportunities Surround US and sometimes we CHOOSE not to HEAL. Sometimes it Hurts too MUCH to (Peel) BACK the layers and (Feel) WHAT's UNDer THere.

Yet WHAT we're not HEALiNG is HurtinG US SomeHow — WHeTHer through ABSENCE, STAGNATION, AVOiDance, or BAD DreAMS.

A BAD DreAM can SNArL UP the air

HEALING can Also FeeL lonely,
especially if we continually FeeL that
we Are the "only ones."

All Alone

I Believe THAT the MORE I SHARE MY
Life and process Honestly, the more I can
HEAL, and, in turn, Help others to HEAL.

we are not alone

HEALING can Be nearly invisible,
Agonizingly slow, Astonishingly rapid, easy,
very Difficult, and inexplicably woven
into the Hurts so we can't tell WHAT'S
Been HEALED right AWAY.

THE very WEAVING HEALS US

We FeeL so terribly Alone in our pain, yet
we Are not. I Know this, Because AS I AM
plowing through OLD Agonizing layers, repeating
patterns and various expressions of not o.k. ness,
I Meet others on the PATH of tears
and HEALING.

13

I see, hear, and sense them in the DARK CAVERNS!

These "DARK CAVERNS" are an inescapable part of our journey, yet we don't need to live there. WE MUST PASS THROUGH and STAY LONG ENOUGH to SIFT THROUGH and FIND OUR WHOLE SELVES.

The entrance is sometimes guarded by fierce creatures

There ARE jewels in the dirt, gifts in the mud, doorways we didn't previously see.
We can trust in these PASSAGEWAYS, in this pain. We can share our excavations and raw searchings with each other.

Mysterious Doorways

I AM SO Honored to see another's true pain or tears (when I'm not too scared).

Hey! Guess WHAT I found?

So many of us think it's not safe or fruitful to share ours.

The Blessings of SHARED Fruit

Yet, whenever we can face pain — our own or another's — our hearts open still more.

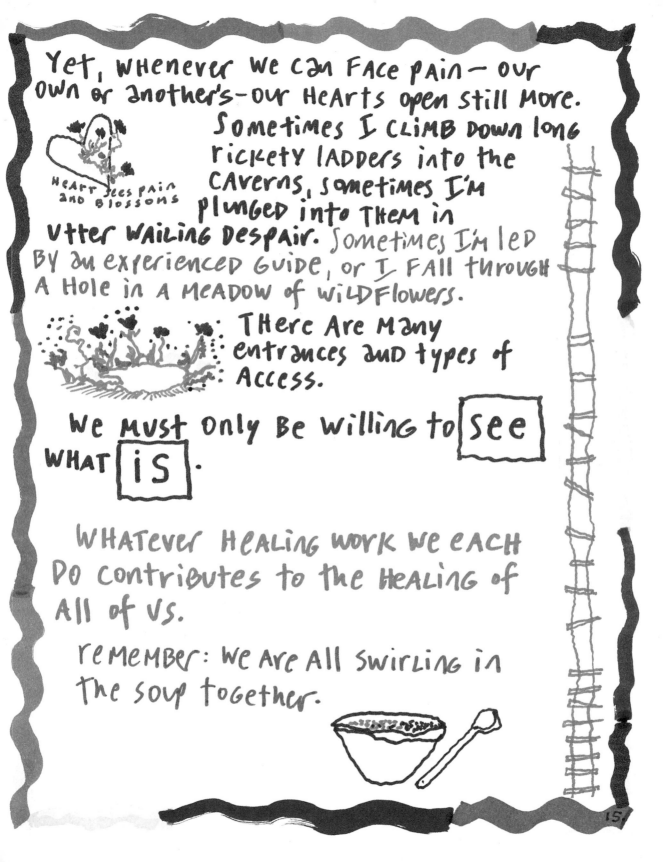

Sometimes I climb down long rickety ladders into the caverns, sometimes I'm plunged into them in utter wailing despair. Sometimes I'm led by an experienced guide, or I fall through a hole in a meadow of wildflowers.

Heart sees pain and blossoms

There are many entrances and types of access.

We must only be willing to see what is .

Whatever healing work we each do contributes to the healing of all of us.

Remember: we are all swirling in the soup together.

I AM not an "expert" on HEALING. I HOLD no Degrees except Degrees of COMPASSION, insanity, and WILD·HEARTEDNESS.

I completed 9 years of psychotherapy, Group and individual, with A DEManDing and insight-Ful Guide. it's A GOOD place to start!

I'm eccentric and ordinary, streaked with 'Garden variety' neurosis.

THis is A Book of Questions and Discoveries.

There are lots of weeds in my Garden

I invite you to reAD SDrAWKCAB, ¡umop ap!sdn, Color the pages, ADD your own Drawings, teAr pAGes out and SHAre THEM with Friends.

There is no order to this Book, rather A Friendly Disorder.

Let's speAK of our secrets, SHAre our pAin and tears, and lean in closely together to peer into the DArK CAverns. We Are so indelibly connected to EACH other, and SUCH tender SOULS. There is MUCH to HEAL and A lot to LAUGH ABOUT.

let's Begin.

MY MOTHER IS NO LONGER THE PROBLEM... NOW WHAT?

For years I blamed all or most of my problems on other people, mostly my mother. I collected evidence of how we didn't get along, and things she had "done to me." Of course, I was also excruciatingly aware of how much love there was between us, and I knew it was necessary to heal this relationship.

I had the chance to heal and complete my relationship with my father before he died, and knew how good it felt to have only love between us. We had cleared up considerable personality conflicts and grudges. I didn't see how the same would be possible with my mother.

We are strikingly similar and yet very different. She sent me a card once of two porcupines trying to hug.

How do they hug?

Very carefully!

ABOUT HALFWAY THROUGH MY nine-year Psychotherapy relationship, I returned to MY CHILDHOOD HOME AND DUG AROUND FOR MORE "evidence" to Present ABOUT HOW I HAD Been ABUSED in that HOUSE. I Prepared FOR MY PHONE therapy session WITH notes OF WHAT I'D DISCOVERED.

MY therapist said,

"THIS is A BIT CONTROVERSIAL, WHAT I'M ABOUT to say. I'M GOING to ASK that We not talk ANYMORE ABOUT your Parents in therapy."

I FELT like I'D FALLEN OUT OF A PLANE WITHOUT A PARACHUTE, AND FINALLY MANAGED to say,

"WHAT WIll WE talk ABOUT then?"

I really DIDN'T KNOW

"We'll talk ABOUT J U S t y o u."

I COULDN'T iMAGINE HOW WE'D FILL UP the time!

I FELT FLUNG into the U N K N O W N

THAT Conversation WAS the BEGINNING OF A DEEP HEALING THAT CONTINUES to this DAY.

And so I stopped blaming my
mother, my brother who drinks, the Lutheran
church, the Minneapolis public school system,
society in general, men in particular,
and anything else I could dream up to
avoid looking at myself.

It's much harder to look at one's self.
Jesus said,

"Stop pointing out the speck in your
friend's eye, and concentrate on the
log in your own."

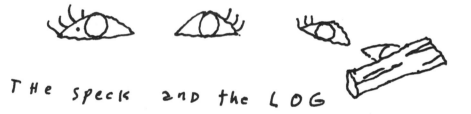

THe speck and the LOG

It doesn't matter what you can find in
another's personality to irritate or
convince you that it's... her ... fault ...
she's ... so ... wrong ... There
will always be copious evidence.

It matters what your responses are.

I work with a healer who has been assisting me in developing objectivity versus reactivity in my responses. I used to L e A p at the slightest offense. (Now I leap to choose again.) I can step out of myself and calmly assess a situation before emotionally re·acting.

I had a chance to test some of my new skills by going on a cruise with my mom and younger brother. We were to spend seven days in a small stateroom together, with a private balcony. I planned on bringing a tent and pitching it on that balcony for some privacy. At the last minute, the tent seemed bulky and I left it at home...

cruise camping

P.s.

Did I mention my tendencies to become seasick, claustrophobic, and highly sensitive to stimuli?

My mom is 76, and I wanted new memories with her. I put aside my "Cruise Fears" and went.

The first night fulfilled all my worst fears: impossibly tiny cabin, almost immediate dehydration and seasickness, and when I called to try to buy more space, I was cheerily informed,

"Sorry, we're completely sold out!"

Just then, I saw the gangplank being pulled back, and the ship moved away from the dock! After I flung myself on the bed crying, I joined my mom and brother at the buffet upstairs.

Did I mention <u>despising</u> buffets?

I slept on a pullout couch near the sliding glass doors open to the sea air. After 10 hours of blissful, rocking sleep, I woke up to blue waters and sky and completely enjoyed <u>All</u> the rest of the cruise! It felt like years of trauma had been healed during the night.

You know what I forgot about fearing spending that much time in a small space with my mother?

HOW MUCH WE love eACH other

My Mother said she had to get home from the Cruise to recover from laughing so much. She Also said she might want to Cruise to Europe next!

I am so grateful to have these new experiences with my Mother.

But what do you do if you're thinking: "That's nice for her, But My Mother still is the Problem!"

Consider trying on a new Belief:

No Matter what
your Mother has
or hasn't Done,
Can you look
only
At yourself?

If not, Why not?

I Assure you that My Mother didn't change that much, (I did.)

There is a tremendous Freedom in Being the one to Change.

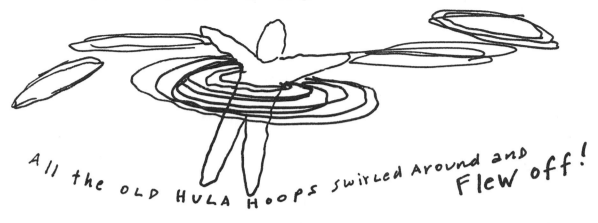

All the old HULA HoopS swirLed Around and Flew off!

It does involve letting go of the Attachments to Justice, revenge, self-righteous Behaviors, and proving past Wrongs. It Also means releasing expectations that <u>you</u> <u>will</u> <u>ever</u> <u>get</u> <u>what</u> <u>you</u> <u>think</u> <u>you</u> <u>missed</u> <u>out</u> <u>on</u> <u>Back</u> then <u>or</u> <u>now</u>.

This type of healing is A spiral Dance that Proceeds through the layers of the Past and Present. You will Falter, Blame Again, return to self-Defeat. You Can Also keep

CHOOSING AGAIN

I AM.

Brambles of Intimacy

What happens when you "Break up" with someone you love? Here's what happened to me. After being in a relationship for 4 1/2 years and thinking we were headed toward marriage, I awakened over a period of time to true feelings of knowing it was "over."

I desperately wanted it to work. It felt like my last chance to be normal.

(Now I laugh writing this, then I cried.)

The worst thing was that we had none of the relationship problems I had encountered before—no glaring, obvious billboards of bad news. This was more subtle, the truth more elusive and the ending more devastating than any I'd ever experienced.

it was not like a billboard

Worse still was the fact that he was slowly becoming my best friend, and that I actually liked him as well as loved him. I tried to lie, first to myself and then to him.

I had never consciously ended a romantic relationship.

It was always covert manipulation or sabotage or never-speaking-to-them-again.

I tried to propose a separation over the phone. Then I called back and asked him to meet me instead.

When I looked into his eyes and told the truth, it was worse than I imagined. We tried to take a walk after talking, but it was like a death march. Finally, I was back in my car, sobbing as I drove slowly on the winding road, repeatedly unfogging the windows.

My Heart Felt Cracked and Shredded

My memory of the days that followed is that they were an unendurable blur. I went to sleep crying and woke up crying. I couldn't breathe deeply, and even my cat couldn't console me.

I am sure that if we ever truly remembered that kind of pain we would never attempt loving someone again. I know that eventually, a certain kind of amnesia takes over and the pain fades with time until we can barely remember it.

After three days apart, he and I spoke on the phone and he said,

"I've been praying, reflecting, and writing in my journal about all of this. I tried to blame you, make you wrong, but I couldn't. I know now that you did the best thing, and I wish you'd had the courage to do it a long time ago."

I cried with relief at the validation of his words, and we made an appointment to see our couple's therapist together. The therapist named the process a "relationship autopsy."

We sifted through the bones and embers of the relationship

I will always be grateful to both of us for taking this step

We sifted through the bones of the relationship to discover where it had died, or if it had. We expressed painful and tender feelings to each other with the assistance of a guide. What a terrifying and helpful process this was.

I SWUNG BETWEEN DESPISING IT AND CRAVING IT.

AT THE END,

it WAS an ODD swing set

there WAS a KIND OF PEACE AND CLOSURE THAT I HADN'T EXPERIENCED BEFORE. I SAW THAT TO CONTINUE OUR RELATIONSHIP OR NOT WAS COMPLETELY OUR CHOICE.

We CHOSE NOT TO CONTINUE.

We THEN TRIED TO BECOME FRIENDS TOO QUICKLY. WHAT A DELICATE MATTER. NOW THERE IS A COMPANIONABLE SILENCE, A RESPECTFULLY DISTANT FRIENDSHIP.

I STILL FEEL PANGS. I ALSO KNOW THAT I AM TRULY AND COMPLETELY LOVING MYSELF FOR THE FIRST TIME, AND THAT IS A FULL-TIME JOB.

I ALSO KNOW THAT WE NEEDED EACH OTHER TO GROW AS WE DID, AND THAT WE NEVER KNOW WHAT A PERSON'S PURPOSE IS IN OUR LIFE, OR HOW LONG HE OR SHE WILL BE IN IT.

TO TRUST IN OUR OWN TRUTH IS THE ONLY WAY.

TRUST

I USED to GET Jealous OF People
Whose love lives seemed easier,
especially if I WAS BUSY idealizing
them!

it's so eAsy For Them... less wounding They HAVE More Money...
BeHer PArents They've never HAD to... More
I BeT They HAve... SHE HAS... BeHer THerApy... ConFidence
THey cAme FRom A FunctionAl FAmily...
He HAS...

the idealizing mind

(critical variety)

Now I know that we all stumble, and
GET scared, And Hide OUT, and Are learning
our lessons in love WHeTHer romantic or
not.

Being A somewHat public Person and
Having WriTTen ABout MY relationship in
two OF MY Books, I sHared the Breakup
on MY inspiration Phone line over A
Period OF MontHs and received Many
tHousands OF AstoUnding Messages OF
support and GraTitude For MY speaking
OF This Particular Kind OF Pain.

4 1 5
5 4 6
3 7 4 2

Bless All of you
WHo CAll
The
inspiration
Line

I find inspiration in pain.
I wish for you:

© Wise, conscious breakups
© The completion of a relationship autopsy
© Being awake in love
© Sharing your pain with others
© The knowledge that you are never alone
© The awareness that pain will change,
   fade, and even end.

We do need a hospital for the brokenhearted.
There would be:

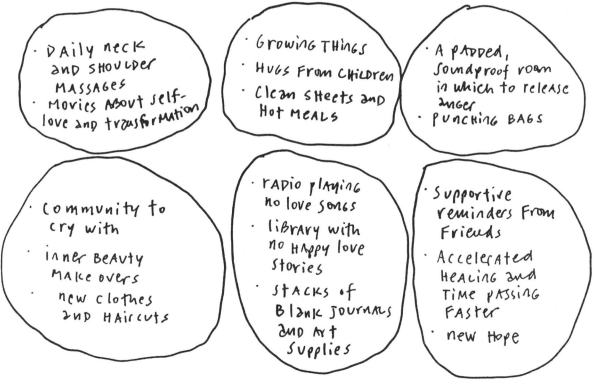

· Daily neck and shoulder massages
· Movies about self-love and transformation

· Growing things
· Hugs from children
· Clean sheets and hot meals

· A padded, soundproof room in which to release anger
· Punching bags

· Community to cry with
· Inner beauty make overs
· New clothes and haircuts

· Radio playing no love songs
· Library with no happy love stories
· Stacks of blank journals and art supplies

· Supportive reminders from friends
· Accelerated healing and time passing faster
· New hope

We Are All Indelibly Connected

I had a dream where I peeled the rooftops off all of the houses and buildings, and peered inside to see how close we really all are.

Those thin walls between all of our beds and soft sleeping bodies.

Maya Angelou reminds us, "I have discovered that we are more alike than unalike as people."

I went to hear Dr. Rachel Naomi Remen, author of Kitchen Table Wisdom, and she said,

"Knowing that your love matters is the foundation on which to build a life."

We forget how much our love matters. We think we travel unseen in this world. Actually, we are all acutely aware of each other.

There is a powerful exercise called "The Good Gossip," which was invented by Barbara Sher, speaker and author of Wishcraft and Live the Life You Love.

She uses it for instant team building. I have witnessed it as instant love raising.

Each team consists of three people who don't know each other.

One person, with pen and paper, turns her back, and takes notes

it's a love-raising experience

As the other two say good things about the third person.

At first, the two are reaching for details they've noticed.

"She has really shiny hair. She seems kind."

Then, it gets more detailed and uncannily accurate. Soon, the third person has filled the sheet with descriptions about herself.

Here is my sheet that I saved from several years ago:

I like her bright colors. I noticed her right away. She seems strong and smart. Maybe she's a teacher or something? She was really listening and laughing a lot too. I bet she's a good friend. She was really sensitive with that child that wouldn't stop talking. I wonder if she's a mom or just naturally good with kids. People seem to like her and ask her questions. She's definitely a leader. Yes and artist of some kind too, I bet. Her clothes and bag are really creative. I noticed her unusual brightly colored ring and that unusual scarf. I just felt safe around her. Like she knows what she's doing. She's really pretty too and I love her haircut! I love how much she laughs. And how loud! She seems really healthy.

IT is ASTOUNDING to WITNESS THIS PROCESS AND EXPERIENCE HOW MUCH WE ALL NOTICE ABOUT EACH OTHER.

IT is so VALIDATING AND LIBERATING to realize HOW WE ARE truly seen even if WE ARE not "KNOWN" in THE FORMAL sense.

WE ARE ALL PSYCHICALLY AND INTUITIVELY GIFTED AND CAN USE THOSE GIFTS to increase OUR sense OF INTIMACY WITH THIS WORLD, AND THE PEOPLE IN IT.

I WANT to remind you OF THE importance OF your spirit and HOW indelibly connected WE ALL ARE.

spirits moving and touching

Our spirits crave union AND WE HAVE MUCH to share WITH EACH OTHER.

Write DOWN THIS sentence somewhere WHERE you CAN see IT OFTEN:

I AM indelibly connected to everyone.

Broken Friendships

Someone Called MY inspiration Phone line and asked me to speak about Broken or Disintegrating Friendships.

MY Friend Debra once said to me, "No one Friend Can Be everything."

I know that I have tried to make Friends into "everything": endlessly supportive, responsive, and understanding.

I have learned that MY Friends are All swirling in the soup with me.

Person Lying Down To rest From Trying to _Be_ everything or Trying to get someone else to _Be_ everything

Sometimes a Friend Cannot "Be there" For me, For reasons that have nothing to do with me! or, I Cannot Be there For Her.

A Friend may Be restimulated or experiencing strong emotions as a result of an interaction Between us and need time to Process and absorb it, or she may just be immersed in her own "stuff."

I Become alarmed at silences or absences and tend to interpret them as abandonments.

I Find myself measuring the love Between us and Fear any slippage or Change.

At These Times I use A Demented Measuring Device

The abandoning is actually being done to me, by me!

We must take time to fight and to feel conflict and anger, not to try to fix it or "be nice" or be-friends-again-no-matter-what.

Oh yes, we can carefully thread our friendships through an intellectual needle and stay away from the messy intimacy that comes with real, long-term friendships. I've used this stagnant method when I was too scared or unskilled to do anything else.

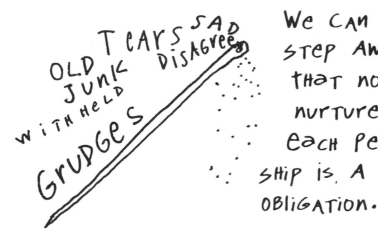

OLD TEARS SAD
JUNK DISAGREE
WITHHELD
GRUDGES

We can also choose to step away from friendships that no longer work or nurture.

Each person's friend-ship is a gift, not an obligation.

Still, if a friendship does end, it makes room for something else to grow.

My friend Elissa calls this "fertile emptiness." In this fertile emptiness can grow a whole new plant that you couldn't even have envisioned before.

A whole new kind of plant

All the new plants form an unusual friendship garden

I know that my 20s and 30s were spent learning the bumps and knots of friendship. My 40s and 50s will be spent allowing friendship in all of its forms and vagaries.

The "breaking" of friendships comes with all of its lessons in allowing and letting go. We cannot make a friendship be something else.

Friendships occur in layers and cycles like all the rest.

We must be our own truest friend.
Our own indelible best friend.

THAT can never be broken

Being Your Own Partner
Marry Yourself

These are two words I wrote in my poster "How to Be really Alive" after I'd had my own wedding ceremony. I've witnessed and shared in many people's stories of self-marriage, and know that it is a rich option.   *so rich*

I'd realized that I had so much self-healing to do, that I really wasn't ready for another person as my partner! Perhaps if I _fully_ became my own partner, I would then be a full vessel meeting another, instead of a starving, empty vessel waiting to be filled. (which is how I had conducted my many relationships in the past.)

in fact, spilling over

I knew what it felt like to be searching for union with another. I had no idea how to give that union to myself. Here are some steps that I took:

(Self·romance:)

How much do you/have you romanced yourself? What dates, trips, seductions, or extravagances have you planned or undertaken?

note: These can be simple, inexpensive, and highly original odd moments of moon watching, wine drinking, sun napping, and dancing by yourself.

(Sexuality/Celibacy:)

How much have you learned about self-loving and of sexuality with yourself/by yourself?

note: Masturbation is an art and a blessing and just loves practice! Have you ever engaged in conscious celibacy?

(Solitude/Aloneness:)

How much time do you/have you spent in conscious aloneness?

note: Solitude and aloneness are different from loneliness and frantic isolation. There is much to learn and experiment with about these various states.

(Self·retreat/Sabbatical/traveling Alone:)

Have you retreated? Planned a sabbatical? Traveled alone? Why or why not?

note: We are strongly encouraged to be social, yet little guidance and support is given for the more solitary practices. This is rapidly changing!

38

Books/relationships

"We Are All stumbling towards the light with varying degrees of grace at any given moment." Bo Losoff

How to Forgive When You Don't Know How
By Jacqui Bishop M.S.
Mary Grunte R.N.

If You Had Controlling Parents
By Dan Neuharth

Imagine a Woman in Love With Herself
By Patricia Lynn Reilly

Creative Visualization
By Shakti Gawain

You Can Heal Your Life
By Louise L. Hay

Operating Instructions
By Anne Lamott

I Know Why the Caged Bird Sings
By Maya Angelou

"The First rule is to keep an untroubled spirit.
The second is to look things in the face
and know them for what they are."
Marcus Aurelius

Terror of Change
(and the Fruits of letting Go)

I am startled by change. I am also energized by it. The "ideal me" gracefully embraces and accepts change. The "real me" most often resists and struggles against it. I am still personally affronted by changes I didn't see coming or can't do anything about, or wouldn't have chosen!

I'm amused by my feeble attempts to change change!

Every time someone says,

"The only thing you can count on is change,"

HOW can we sit with change?

I am secretly horrified: yet I, too, count on change! I seek it out and nurture its existence. When asked, "What's new?" I could talk for a week.

It's embarrassing to admit that I love change when it suits or benefits me, or the world, or those I love. Change that I don't understand alarms me.

I think it is very seductive to form
a picture in your mind of how it will be,
or how you would like it to be, and then
frantically try to apply that picture to
what is actually happening.

Fantasy picture

Actual picture

I remind myself that my "pictures" are
merely the faintest maps by which to
navigate.

I still have difficulty trusting in the
"Divine Plan."   What if the Divine is Misguided?

The "fruits of letting go" come when I can truly
see that I Am not in Charge, and that I can
trust in the divinity and process of change.

Then I relax and feel myself buoyed
and swept along by the changes themselves.

it can be very liberating to let go and be
SWEPT ALONG

The sweet fruits are obtained by
bending and stretching to accommodate
change, to bless and to welcome it,
and ultimately to trust in the utter simplicity
of change as actual life.

So many times, I see the change I railed against as the perfect choice for me now.

I have no advice or suggestions for dealing with change, since I feel supremely incompetent and relentlessly resistant to it.

So I live in a paradox, in a common human condition perhaps called: responding to change.

I seek neutrality and learning to become my own calm anchor more and more as my changes multiply.

CHaNGe	$
new Attitude	1
letting Go	1
leap of Faith	1
CHaNGes	
GALore	

A new kind of change machine!

I want to talk about change and hear how others experience and live with change.

I intend to learn to live fully with all of my changes.

I offer this quote by the photographer Ruth Bernhard from her "Recipe for a long and happy life"

#1. never get used to anything

I now welcome and embrace changes in my life. Ha!

42

Money and How we Suffer About it

We All Have A Money story. We Have Money traumas, triumphs, lessons, and History. We Have Money styles. Money is A subject to Be studied with enthusiasm and commitment, yet We All turn AWAY From seeing our Money story As it Actually is. We Avoid thinking About How we'd Actually like it to Be!

We need to (WAKE UP) our Money exploring selves.

I attended A workshop one time, and found out that my two predominant needs regarding Money Were Freedom and security. This Baffled Me For Many years. I Couldn't Figure out How the two could coexist! Now I Am Beginning to see. I watch Myself Avoid, ABdicate, Make Hasty or reckless decisions regarding Money, or I Find Myself Wishing that "someone else Would do it," or that it Would Just MAGically Get Done.

I Haven't really Grown up my Money self.

Money is a tool we must use through our entire lives, yet we are not taught about money in schools in a basic and helpful way, using real-life situations.

THIS keeps us very young
about money

Thankfully, you can get conscious and clear assistance about money, as many of us face new decisions about money in our lives.

Time to Grow UP
our money selves

Try this:

(Declare the year 2000) to be a healing money experiment

Create a healing circle.

it can be you and one other person

My friend andrea participates in a group called (in-progress) which assists the members in creative goals. Consider forming an in-progress circle about money.

Share questions, ideas, frustrations, and avoidances about (money.)

I'm going to be doing this. let's compare money notes.

Money   Flows   To new   places

Stupid, Lonely, and Broke

You Are either in this Place, Have Been in this place, or Are not Currently in this place and Can reach out to Help those that May Be.

I Am stupid and lonely Most Days in some WAY. I Am Broke Most often in spirit, or in increasing MY Abundance, or Broke in sharing With others.

We Are terrified of Words like these, and of the states of Being they Portray.

We Are constantly reminded By Society that this is What could Happen if...

We slip and Fall, Don't Pay Attention, or Keep A steady Job or Become reckless.

We Don't WANT to linger in the Dark Woods of these Words, or even visit there if We CAN Help it.

THE DARK WOODS CAN SCARE US

When I was a "starving artist," I was abundant in so many other ways. Now that I have more material wealth, I must be conscious to share it and not let it eclipse my spiritual wealth.

When I am trying to be so smart, I must remember my stupidity, my many blindnesses, my incredible arrogance.

I must not cover up my loneliness with distractions or successes or adoring readers. I must sit with the pain of loneliness and learn from it.

I AM loneliness I AM in your mind and body I can get really LARGE

sitting with loneliness

I am broke anytime I turn away from the flow of spirit and forget to trust in life itself.

Being stupid, lonely, and broke has no power or shame other than the extent to which we turn away from it, judge others, or judge ourselves.

JUDGMENT JAR

THe WeiGHT of Isolation

We Are Convinced We Are totally Alone. We Know tHat we Are the ONLY ONes Feeling tHis Crazy, Sick, lost, or Broken.

Being isolated CAN Be terrifying. often we self-impose tHis Condition. Being Alone is Full of Gifts. Solitude CAN Be A Wonder. You CAN study its different states and learn How you participate or Avoid participating. I love tHe AutHor Stephanie Dowrick, WHo says,

"WitHout some Acceptance of that 'essential Aloneness' WHich is Part of the HumaN Condition, the experience of Closeness (to others) is often difficult."

The Feeling of isolation is A trick, an illusion of tHe ego tHat Convinces Us We Don't Deserve CommuNion.

I Pray tHat every isolated Person Be Able to reacH out, and tHat eacH one of Us study our own isolation and Be Able to spend time witH slower or More isolated People, WHo DoN'T KNoW As MucH ABout reacHing out to others.

"Cluster togetHer like stars."
Henry Miller

Meet Me in the Dark Caverns, Crying

The Poet Gary Rosenthal Writes
Beautifully About this in A poem titled
"In the Museum of the Lord of Shame"
Here is An excerpt:

"and so, when we get close
to the wound, when we cross
the border into Egypt
and begin to get close
to where the secrets Are buried,
our nervous system hears A voice
and the voice says,
'you don't really want to go down there'
And you really don't.
Anymore than Orpheus wanted to go down
the dark staircase
where cobwebs pulse
like trampolines
Upon which the ghosts of houseflies
try to leap out of this world
But what you need
to reclaim
lives down there
South
of your predictable borders
where the soul is
encrusted in salt
From the tears we've yet to shed"

From The Museum of the Lord of Shame © Gary Rosenthal
reprinted with permission from Point Bonita Books

To order Gary Rosenthal's marvelous new book of ecstatic love poems, The you that is everywhere call 1-800-429-1112. You can Also order the Museum of the Lord of Shame chapbook At this number.

We try so hard to live on the bright
surface of things.

When I spoke
of the incest I
suffered, my
family said to me,

"OH, I'M ⟨Fine⟩"

bRight suRface and what lives beneath it

"Why do you want to go back there? It
was all so long ago..."

To some part of my soul, it is as
though it happened today, or yesterday.
They have done Kirlian photography
of the human body and seen handprints
from abuse still show up after many,
many years.

Until I went deep into the caverns,
I could not be free of shame or
memories, or flashbacks, or any of
the symptoms that appeared on
the bright surface.

Do we really have
to go?

The child parts of us need our
support and care at these times

No matter how
many times I
visit these deep
and dark caverns,
I still would
rather not go
down there.

In the dark caverns live healing
secrets and balms for parts of ourselves
worn ragged by the bright surface.

Tiny bits crawling along

We can move like slugs there, nearly
blind and naked, inching along with
microscopic patience and attention for
our deformed or unattractive parts.

We do not escape the darkness by trying
to put time between ourselves and pain by
saying, "Oh well, it was all so long ago..."

Time merely provides an illusory
distance that can prevent us from
doing the necessary work. Time
can actually cause a "scabbing over"
of deep wounds that need
exploration to heal. Perhaps then, death
becomes the tearing off of these
scabbed over places and slows
our reunion with the light.

I do know that the darkness
can shelter our wounded places
until we're ready to bring
them into the light.

Lantern of
readiness

Your willingness to visit the dark caverns is all that's needed. You don't need to know how to do anything except search without knowing, and allow your findings.

Meet me in the dark caverns, crying. I'll be there, with all of my resistance and avoidance.

I'll be searching for, and allowing, the healing.

"You do not need to know precisely what is happening, or exactly where it is all going. What you need is to recognize the possibilities and challenges offered by the present moment, and to embrace them with courage, faith and hope."
— Thomas Merton

Meet me in the dark caverns crying. Pick up a flashlight at the entrance

Flash Lights

Books / What Hurts?

"The mind thinks thoughts that
we don't plan. It's not as if we say,
'At 9:10 I'm going to be filled with self-hatred.'"
Sharon Salzburg

When Things Fall Apart
Start Where You Are   By Pema Chödrön

Soul Retrieval
            By Sandra Ingerman and Michael Harner

Stay Close and Do Nothing   By Merrill Collett

Sex and Money... Are Dirty, Aren't They?
The Fear Book
The Depression Book   By Cheri Huber

The Healing Choice: Your Guide to Emotional
Recovery After An Abortion
            By Candace DePuy and Dana Dovitch

Intimacy and Solitude   By Stephanie Dowrick

Seven Stages of Money Maturity   By George Kinder

The You That Is Everywhere: love Poems
            By Gary Rosenthal
            To order, call (800) 429-1112

"May you be blessed into usefulness."
Dalai Lama

WHY DO WE CARE ABOUT CHIN HAIR?

One of the bravest and funniest things I ever saw was Rosie O'Donnell, on her talk show, come out with a long chin hair with a bead at the end of it.

It was horrifying, fascinating, hysterically funny, and very revolutionary.

Why do we care so much about these things? I think we fear evidence of imperfection in our bodies and our lives.

I think we care because they are physical evidence of imperfections we perceive in our character, our mortality, and of nature's claims on us.

We perceive chin hair to be an unsightly imperfection and hope that no one ever notices or finds out that we have it.

Of course we forget that all people have random hairs all over their bodies!

We are not less attractive because of chin, breast, ear, leg, or armpit hairs.

if the body is a garden, perhaps these hairs are like dandelions

I WAS GOING to HAVE MY Cellulite PHOTOGRAPHED FOR this BOOK. THEN I realiZED THAT IT WOULD BE GIVING IT MORE IMPORTANCE THAN IT DESERVES.

COULD I POSSIBLY BE...

ACCEPTING Cellulite?

Healing From the SHAME OF IT?

I AM so GRATEFUL to HAVE FUNCTIONING leGs! Yes, I WOULD raTHer HAVE SMOOTH, Cellulite-Free Ones, BUT I WOULD Also raTHer HAVE SMAll Breasts or Dark SKIN or?

I AM A WORK-in-PROGRESS.

I AM UNDER CONSTRUCTION/RENOVATION.

I AM SUBLIMELY, eXACTly HOW I neeD to BE AT THIS MOMENT.

I AM DETERMINED to ACCEPT the Cellulite, the CHIN AND BREAST Hairs, and ANY OTHER BODILY IMPERFECTIONS and in FacT, CELEBRATE THEM!

woman celebrates lumpiness

54

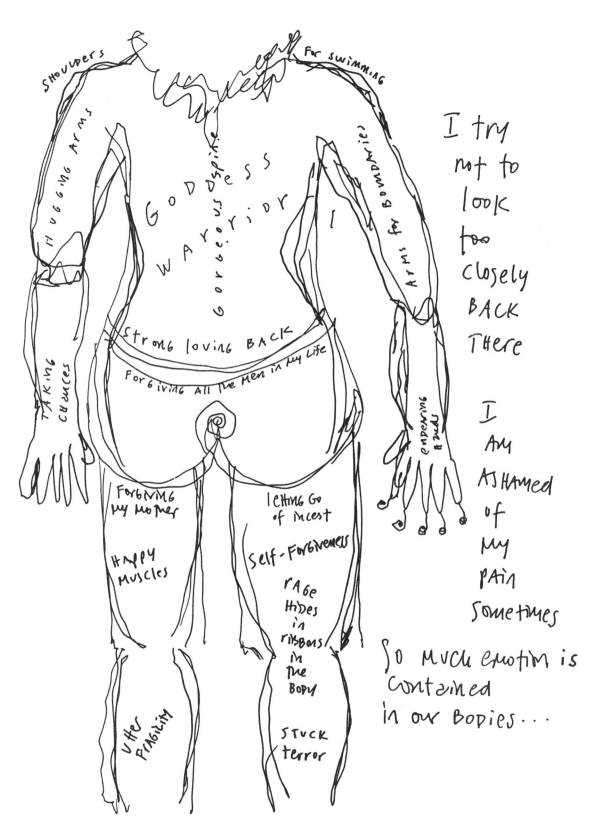

I try not to look too closely BACK There

I AM ASHAMED of MY PAIN Sometimes

So MUCH emotion is Contained in our Bodies...

55

I GET SAD WHEN I SEE WOMEN'S BODIES UNTREASURED, UNACCEPTED, AND IN REVOLT AGAINST THEMSELVES. I GET SAD WHEN I DO THIS.

I remember MY therapist saying, "You need to love the fat Girl in you, too."

BUT I HADN'T. WHEN I GAINED WEIGHT, I HATED THE FAT GIRL! I STILL HAVE remnants OF THIS HATE. I STILL FEEL BETTER WHEN I'M thinner or more "in shape." Some of this Feels HEALTHY, some DOES NOT.

I DID A DRAWING once titled "DIETING ELEPHANT."

IT IS MY STATEMENT OF HOW ANIMALS ARE ALL SORTS OF SIZES, SHAPES, AND HEIGHTS.

DIETING ELEPHANT

WHERE IS COMPASSION AND RESPECT FOR OUR DIFFERENCES?

WHY DO WE CARE SO MUCH ABOUT WHO'S FAT AND WHO'S NOT?

WE DON'T TURN AWAY FROM HIPPOS BECAUSE OF THEIR SIZE, YET WE TURN AWAY FROM FAT OR BIG HUMANS. There is SOMETHING PERVERSE AND insane ABOUT this.

Healing From Trying to Get Well

So often, we reject being sick and perceive it to be bad and very unwelcome. There is never "time to be sick." We are horrified at what feels like betrayal of our bodies, or weakness, or what seems like loss: of energy, of fun, of our perception of our good health.

Being sick = BAD   Being Healthy = Good

I JUST heard this quote:
"Did we ever think the reason we can't find a cure for the common cold is that the common cold is the cure?"

Also, trying to get well is like trying to get somewhere.

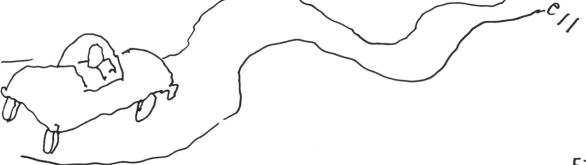

How can we have greater acceptance of our physical bodies and the messages it's sending? Some people take this concept to an extreme, and say that you deserve whatever illness you have, that every disease is self-created.

A blind woman was asked,

"What do you think you didn't want to see that caused you to manifest blindness?"

"People like you," she replied.

There is room to examine the perfection of sickness and the gifts and lessons it brings us.

When we are succulently sick, we will be able to hear the language of the sickness that is speaking through our bodies.

We wake up, pale and creased, hair flat. The world has lost its color temporarily.

Our minds race with the muddy thoughts
of those lost in illness.
Surrender is the message. We don't easily hear
this. We try to escape through denial,
overdoing, or not asking for help.
We keep trying not to surrender.

I can
do it
all
my self

I am just emerging from an illness
as I write this. I spent most of the time
resisting, avoiding, and then trying to eradicate
the symptoms.

> Finally I just
> got quiet
> and listened.

Then I laid flat and quiet for several days.
One morning, the illness had left. I also have
experienced chronic illness that goes on for
weeks, months, years.

"The gods visit us through illness."

Carl Jung

Christiane Northrup, M.D., reminds us in her book,
Women's Bodies, Women's Wisdom, "...I've come to
believe that we can benefit emotionally, physically,
and spiritually by paying attention to our body's
messages."

I know that when I can accept my
symptoms as the language my body speaks in, much
healing and transformation can take place.

59

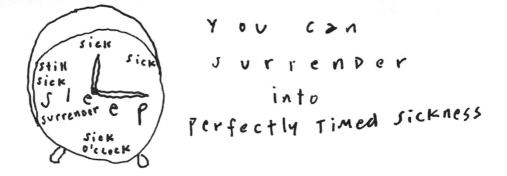

You can Surrender into perfectly timed sickness

I like to say to people when they're ill:

This is the perfect time to be sick

If we can relax and be sick when we don't feel well, we are being present for our actual experience.

Then of course, there are the joys of sickness:

Surrender and collapse, solitude, the bed as nest, sympathy, time to read, quitting doing, solace of visits and friends, and the euphoria of recovery and intense gratitude for good health.

exercising and playing in our bodies

IT seems like such A cruel trick that exercise feels so good only After doing it, And sometimes During it. (Before) doing it is the chasm to be crossed.

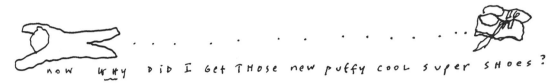

now why DID I get those new puffy cool super shoes?

MY BODY says "move" And MY MIND says "lie Down." I've Been very inspired By MY Friend Brigette And her Practice OF YOGA. She said to Me,

"I JUST SHOW UP. I Don't think About HOW it will Be When I get there."

Aha! I had Been spending Copious Amounts of energy imagining HOW-IT-WOULD-BE-WHEN-I-GOT-THERE. I WAS involved in so Many Mechanisms OF Preparation that now I'M not surprised that I Became sedentary.

it WAS All too exHAusting To THink ABout

The subject of exercise is also a favorite of the inner critics. The voices of mine sound something like this:

"Oh, why even start? You always quit anyway."

READ inner critic Books by Hal & Sidra Stone PH.D

"You'll never see any real progress."

"Other people have better routines, clothes, attitudes, commitment levels, and skills."

"Have you seen your butt lately?"

"Why are you really doing this?"

These misguided voices started as protectors, and now specialize in warnings and fears. They need to be redirected, given new jobs, and turned into allies. I'm now allowing these voices to lead the way:

"I'm so proud of you for just going!"

"Look at all the improvements you've made in just a few months."

"You look like you're glowing."

"Congratulations for just showing up."

"I can really see the commitment you've made."

As I work at turning Critics into Allies,
I notice subtle new levels of Criticism.
For instance, I tend to panic if illness or
inertia interrupts my "schedule." "Now you'll
never catch up!" (Never mind that I've only
had a schedule of exercise for the last six
months!)

"It's all about continuing to show up and
renewing body movement every day in some way

and if not every day, then when I am able to."
Or, as my friend PATRICIA SAYS,
"Learn to compassionately partner with your body."

We've all begun and quit, quit and
begun again.

every tiny thing counts

BOUNCING

Nobody is motivated all the time
(or if she is, she is probably annoying).
Let's move our bodies in new and
joy·full ways.

BALLS

Let's smile and laugh as we
move and breathe.

Let's try new physical things.

·f
JOY

63

Let's play more games together.

Let's stretch more than our muscles.

I was at the gym the other day and they have these colorful big rubber exercise balls.

Also, find out who you are when not exercising

I started bouncing on one and couldn't stop! Pretty soon, I was bouncing and laughing to the point where other people started laughing too as they stretched. Now I include bouncing and laughing in my "routine."

My brother Andrew came with me one night and I asked him to help me do a handstand.

Break Free of Having A routine

I couldn't do it without his support, and kept screaming as I got into the position. It felt so energizing and hilarious. I don't think that our bodies care what or how we move, just that we do move.

I'm going to continue to move gently in new and nourishing ways. I plan to:
- Do a handstand and headstand
- Do a back bend
- Continue stretching my spine
- Try a yoga class or find a teacher
- return to pilates (yes stella!)
- resume weight training

I did one while writing this!

I want to find ways to encourage my gym to add programs of fun physical movement to inspire me.

I WISH

For All of us

Joy Full

movement

and acceptance of not moving times

Food and Where it leads us

I was a secret Binge eater. I kept this secret, not just from other people, but from myself. Oh, there were clues: when I joined OA (overeaters Anonymous), when I would avidly read checklists in Magazines titled: "Are you Addicted to Compulsive eating?" and I would see on the list

   ✓ Do you hide or hoard food?

   ✓ Do you secretly plan to eat?

   ✓ Do you use food as a substitute
      for emotions?

I had voluminous evidence. But still, my Binge eating was tightly controlled, carefully regulated, and never involved large quantities of food. Although I guess the word L A R G E was open to interpretation.

 There Are people who won't customarily eat an entire row of cookies, or hear food calling their name from other rooms, or who don't grind up food in the garbage disposal for fear of eating it, or get it back out of the garbage so they could eat it.

Of course, my binge eating was just a cover-up for the larger issue:

Trying to fill the emptiness

My mother gained weight after having children and quitting smoking. She used to say, "Well, I may be fat, but my children won't be."

I remember being a "picky eater" and vowing to never be fat and displease my mother.

Here I am at seven, trying to disappear...

In college, I gained weight for the first time since puberty. I saw a photo of myself in jeans and was shocked at how

hefty-stocky-chunky-thick-big I looked.

It's a little scary to look at photos of me during that time and see the size I actually was.

Through most of my 20s I exercised and ate obsessively, and exhibited anorexic behavior.

In my 30s, I began steadily gaining weight, especially after a chronic heel pain condition drastically altered my exercise habits.

Then it finally happened.

I was fat.

OH NO

Again, I remembered my therapist saying to me, "You need to be able to love the fat girl too."

But I didn't. I was raging and binging and hiding and only wearing black leggings and big shirts.

Slowly, compassion bloomed. Over a period of years, an agonizing process of r a d i c a l   s e l f - A c c e p t a n c e took place.

COMPASSION Bloomed slowly

I stopped trying to eradicate the fat, and stopped all the blaming and stuffing and hiding.

Then I curled up and cried for a very long time

I BEGAN TO ACCEPT MYSELF

AS IS

and not <u>WHEN</u> I GOT THINNER, MORE
FLEXIBLE... ANY OF IT.

it WAS THEN THAT self·love COULD TRULY
B l o s s o m

This spread to other People too. I noticed
THAT I WAS KINDER AND MORE PATIENT
TOWARD ALL SORTS OF PEOPLE WHO HAD
PREVIOUSLY IRRITATED ME.

I HAD STOPPED JUDGING AND CRITICIZING
MYSELF AND OTHERS IN THE SAME HARSH,
REPETITIVE WAYS.

Then, I WAS INSPIRED AND READY TO EXPERIMENT
WITH MY EATING HABITS, AND OVER THE COURSE
OF A YEAR, CHANGED THEM DRAMATICALLY.

it WAS VERY SLOW AND DRAMATIC
AND THE TIMING HAD TO BE JUST RIGHT...

I WAS FINALLY ABLE to PUT DOWN the COMPULSIVE eating AND FACE ALL the FEELINGS THAT ROSE UP IN ITS PLACE.

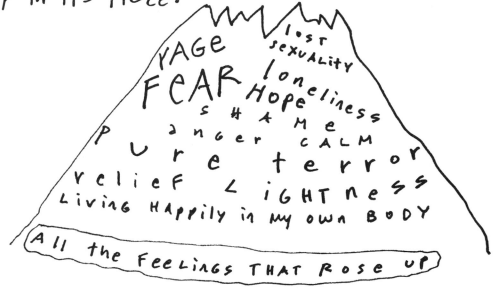

I BEGAN EXERCISING MY BODY DELIBERATELY AND IN ORDER to SWEAT AND BREATHE MORE OXYGEN. AT FIRST JUST 5 to 10 MINUTES, THEN GRADUALLY to 20, 30, AND NOW SOMETIMES 45 MINUTES. I BEGAN WEARING JEANS AND TUCKING MY SHIRTS IN. I SHOPPED FOR BELTS AND BEGAN to LIKE PHOTOGRAPHS OF MYSELF.

The resulting "WEIGHT LOSS" IS REALLY JUST A SIDE EFFECT OF MY OTHER INTERIOR CHANGES.

I'M GrATeful every single DaY for
MY CurrenTlY inacTive eaTing DisorDer,
anD aM FilleD WiTH CoMPassion For
Anyone WHo is exPeriencing iT.

I AM DeePlY saDDeneD to see
BeauTiful WoMen or Men live in Prisons
of fear, faT, anD fooD.

I fiercelY CeleBraTe All the
DifferenT sHaPes AnD siZes AnD PraY
THaT We see the BeauTY in the DiversiTY.

My BroTHer AnDrew saiD to Me,
"I'M GlaD I'M noT like A WoMan WHo
eaTs An Apple AnD THen WonDers if
Her BuTT GoT faTTer."

it's ToTAllY nuTs

I PraY for Peace AnD freeDoM for
WoMen in THeir BoDies anD the ProfounD
Honor THese BoDies Deserve.

suCCulenT WilD WArrior WoMen

Imagine a Woman

Imagine a woman who believes it is right and good she is a woman. A woman who honors her experience and tells her stories. Who refuses to carry the sins of others within her body and life.

Imagine a woman who trusts and respects herself. A woman who listens to her needs and desires. Who meets them with tenderness and grace.

Imagine a woman who has acknowledged the past's influence on the present. A woman who has walked through her past. Who has healed into the present.

Imagine a woman who authors her own life. A woman who exerts, initiates and moves on her own behalf. Who refuses to surrender except to her truest self and wisest voice.

Imagine a woman who names her own gods. A woman who believes her body is enough, just as it is. Who celebrates her body's rhythms and cycles as an exquisite resource.

Imagine a woman who honors the body of the Goddess in her changing body. A woman who celebrates the accumulation of her years and her wisdom. Who refuses to use her precious life energy disguising the changes in her body and life.

Imagine a woman who values the women in her life. A woman who sits in circles of women. Who is reminded of the truth about herself when she forgets.

Imagine yourself as this woman.

By Patricia Lynn Reilly

From _Imagine A Woman in Love With Herself_
reprinted with kind permission from Patricia Lynn Reilly.

Aging... Embracing and Avoiding

I'm not as afraid of <u>being</u> old as much as I'm frightened to experience the process of getting there.

READ:

Be Full of Yourself by Patricia Lynn Reilly

So far, I'm mostly in denial and avoidance. I can't quite comprehend that I'm a "nearly middle-aged woman" at age 45. Of course I plan to live to 120, WHY NOT 300? So "middle age" would start later. I want to be someone who ages graciously and consciously, yet I seem to be stumbling, crawling, and moving to actually being older, with all kinds of resistance.

There is a dating service in San Francisco that told me that they secretly don't accept women over 50, but men up to 70! OUTRAGEOUS

Some of my role models - Katharine Hepburn, Ruth Gordon, Martha Graham - can't help because they're <u>already</u> old, or dead.

Maybe I need an aging support group, although I haven't found people really wanting to acknowledge

I will form a group!

or talk about it. Mostly it's (me) that doesn't want to. It can all seem so dreadfully sad and morbid and so interwoven with C H A N G E.

I've been noticing that I surround myself with people in their 20s and 30s and then sometimes envy their young skin, energy levels, or whatever else I judge to be younger than me.

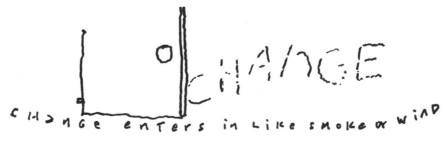

let's talk more about aging!

Yet of course I don't want to actually _be_ younger, without all of my accumulated experiences and yearnings.

I am grateful for every second of my life, and usually don't even consider my age. Still, there is change involved in aging and I am trying to seal off the entry points.

CHANGE

change enters in like smoke or wind

74

The evidence of my aging I
have seen so far:

- When I get dressed up to go out, I feel oddly invisible and not attractive in the ways I used to rely upon.
- Waiters always call me ma'am.
- My lipstick bleeds.
- The crow's feet have a heavier step.
- I feel too old for certain clothing in department stores.
- I am mistaken for being the mother of my younger friends.
- My hair is slightly thinner.
- I rely more on my glasses.
- My own mother is older.

Large crows feet

It's an embarrassing relief to write of these things.

The benefits and gifts of my aging I've seen so far:

- Men or women playing games don't even vaguely interest me.

- MY CenTeRedness and Power.
- I have more insurance and different kinds of Garbage Bags.

i DiDn'T Used to Be Able to Afford very Many Things Like Garbage Bags

- MY vision for helping others is much Clearer and keener.
- I Am less self-Absorbed.
- I Am more Grateful for health and more Compassionate in General.
- I know what I like and how to experience it.   I love This
- Emotional Balance.
- Freedom from reproduction and Childbirth.
- Being Aunt and Godmother and friend to Children.
- Being fiercely in love with myself.
- Being Able to more Deeply Give and receive love.

Maya Angelou says,
    "Oh, MY seventies Are rockin'!"

One night I was lamenting About the Aging Process to my younger Brother Andrew. He Calmly looked At me And said, "What did you think WAS Going to Happen?"   OH DeAr.

My friend Rebecca Latimer, who is 94 and wrote You're Not Old Until You're Ninety... Best to Be Prepared, However said recently,

"As you Age, your body will change a lot and you need to be prepared for it."

My friend Patricia reminded me,

"Aging is a choice and an art form."

And so, as I head toward my 50th year, I will scoop up life even better than before.

I will write and speak about my aging process and not turn away from it.

Scoop up Life

I invite you to join me.

Let's Dance with Time!

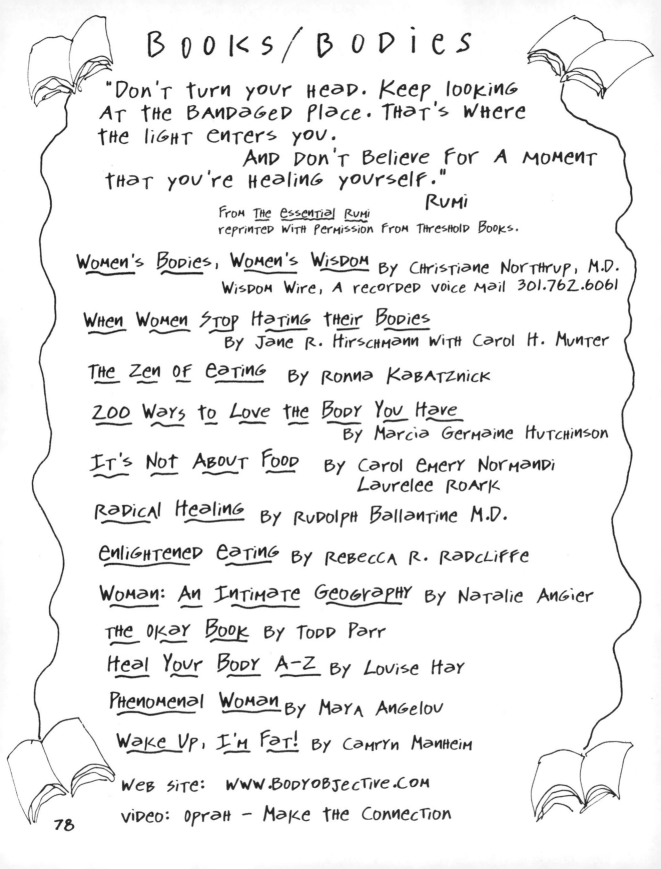

BOOKS/BODIES

"Don't turn your head. Keep looking
At the BANDAGED place. That's where
the light enters you.

           And don't Believe for A moment
that you're healing yourself."
                                    RUMI
From The Essential Rumi
reprinted with Permission from Threshold Books.

Women's Bodies, Women's Wisdom By Christiane Northrup, M.D.
           Wisdom Wire, A recorded voice Mail 301.762.6061

When Women Stop Hating their Bodies
           By Jane R. Hirschmann with Carol H. Munter

The Zen of Eating By Ronna Kabatznick

200 Ways to Love the Body You Have
                 By Marcia Germaine Hutchinson

It's Not About Food By Carol Emery Normandi
                 Laurelee Roark

Radical Healing By Rudolph Ballantine M.D.

Enlightened Eating By Rebecca R. Radcliffe

Woman: An Intimate Geography By Natalie Angier

The Okay Book By Todd Parr

Heal Your Body A-Z By Louise Hay

Phenomenal Woman By Maya Angelou

Wake Up, I'm Fat! By Camryn Manheim

Web site: www.bodyobjective.com

Video: Oprah - Make the Connection

Healing Things To Try

- Call yourself on voice mail And thank yourself for something you did, then save the message And listen later when you've almost forgotten you did it.

- Pay Bills With Brightly Colored Pens And use "good stamps" to mail them.

- Drive A Car lovingly And Gently. Recognize the other Drivers As versions of yourself or of your Best Friend.

- Read About And look At Pictures of treehouses.

- Use A Magnifying Glass to look into the hearts of flowers.

- experiment With Flower essences. BACH is GOOD

- Turn your Bed or Couch into A nap Hut With A fabric roof And supplies inside.

- When you Feel A lot of Feelings, or Just one potent one, (STOP) and Just Feel it so self·intimacy can come.

        STOP and FEEL

- Host a poetry tea with volumes of Maya Angelou, Marge Piercy, e. e. cummings, Shel Silverstein, or a brand-new poet.
- Have more 10-minute chair massages.
- Visit produce sections just to admire fruits and vegetables
- Buy half-price flowers and absorb their beauty quickly.
- Stop making your bed and admire the landscape of sheet.
- Start making your bed and discover the satisfaction of a brand-new bed every time.
- Buy art supplies for children. Any school will welcome the help!
- Rent or borrow a convertible and drive it with no hat or scarf.

- Adopt a school class and visit to share ordinary stories of your life.
- Allow yourself to play the piano with no skill or self-judgment.
- Seek out old people and listen to what they're saying.
- Start a movement in your neighborhood to meet each other.
- Establish a free, trade, or barter box where you live.
- Put iridescent glitter in your bath.
- Serve chilled chocolate chip cookie dough for dessert.
- Listen to more violins!

MY GOD BOX

I FIRST HEARD ABOUT GOD BOXES FROM THE AUTHOR ANNE LAMOTT, WHEN SHE wrote ABOUT HER experiences of MAKING and USING one. I IMMEDIATELY THOUGHT, "THAT'S nice For HER, it will never WORK FOR ME." WHY DO WE think LIKE this? I think WE DO it to PUSH AWAY the FEAR THAT it Won't "WORK for ME" insteAD of JUST opening our HEARTS to it.

SO, I FinAlly MADE one. It turned out to Be an OLD CiGAR BOX THAT JUST "HAPpened" to SAY HEAVEN on A laBEL on The Side. I THOUGHT it MIGHT increase MY CHances of reACHiNG GOD.

GOD'S MAILBOX HAS A PiCKUP every Second

I Began writing Funny Little notes to GOD and slipping them into MY GOD BOX.

Funny Little notes

On oddly shaped

pieces of paper

I

wasn't fussy

A couple of curious things Began to Happen. First, I was able to release obsessive thoughts once I had put a note into the GOD Box, and Mysterious remedies to problems appeared after I'd left a note.

Most importantly, I didn't feel as alone with my problems. I even Began taking requests from certain people for specific problems.

The notes have evolved over time. Instead of material requests or directions to GOD (HA!), I mostly describe various states of surrender and ask for help in experiencing it.

Dear God,
Please Help me to Accept and respond with love to My money fears.
love,
Susan

. NOW MY GOD BOX is entwined in MY LiFe and I turn to it often. once in a while, it Becomes full and I ceremoniously Burn the Little notes and send THE SMOKE up For   HEALING.

I FELT SHY ABout writing this Because I still straDDle the CHristian and BuDDHist worLDs and Don't want to Misrepresent myself AS A CHristian.

I TAKe Heart From WHAT MAYA Angelou SAYS WHen people tell Her they're CHristians. SHe SAYS SHe thinks, "ALReADY? THey're CHristians ALreADY? It seems to Me to Be A Lifetime of worK."

Me and GOD and A Little wooDen Box in San Francisco. I see it AS MY FAiTH in Action in THis one WAY.

85

angels are all around us

angels are doing their
healing work for you. stand
still and let them swirl around
Y   O   U

HEALING OCCURS UNDER THE COVERS

Let sleep Heal You

Transformation Game

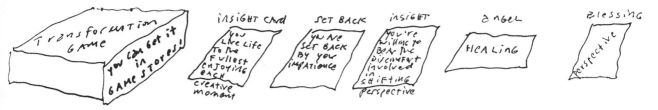

Kathy Tyler and Joy Drake deserve to be honored and acknowledged for their healing work with a series of games, cards, and tools for "the way you play your life."

They lived at a spiritual community in Scotland called Findhorn for many years and developed their work through the living of life and all of its lessons.

I describe the Transformation Game as a therapy session, massage, and tarot reading all in one. The business version of the Transformation Game led to my forming my company, Camp SARK, in 1993.

I use the Intuitive Solutions, Blessing, and Angel cards almost every day.

I find a lot of support and healing in this work and can heartily recommend it to you, and share these resources.

Innerlinks
P.O. Box 10502
Asheville, NC 28806
(828) 665-9937
www.innerlinks.com

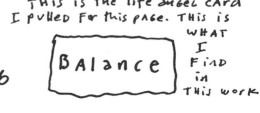

This is the life angel card I pulled for this page. This is WHAT I find in this work

BALANCE

Mirror Work

Try this: Stare into A
Mirror for Many Moments
Without preparing to go somewhere,
or see "How you look," or fix your hair,
look at your skin, or put on makeup.

See what you see. AS iS.

I usually see sadness or resignation
or rage or forced perkiness or signs
of clenching, resisting, or avoiding.
Sometimes I try to adjust the "mask,"
which appears to have slipped.

THE FALLEN MASK

Then I usually
Go Deeper

I speak to Myself
in the Mirror and say,

How Are you, really?

Then, I usually Begin to cry.

I cry until the tears transform into something else.

Sometimes it takes a long time, and I feel sad for most of a day or night.

I used to fear that the tears would never stop.

Now I know that they will.

Mirror work connects us with our essence, the part of us that has never been damaged. I think that the soul just waits for us to notice the sadness and honor it. The honoring releases us to experience other feeling states.

other feeling states

My goddaughter Zoe, age 4 3/4, said to me recently,

"Susan, why don't you just <u>be</u> how you actually <u>are</u>!"

THANKS ZOE

Mirror work reconnects me to be how I actually am, even if I'm trying to rush away from my self, or tell lies, or try to hide.

The mirror doesn't fake it.

Embark on a mirroring journey. . .

let me know what you see

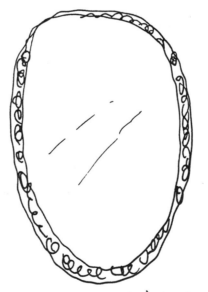

one time I turned into a hawk

Books/Healing Tools

"When one door of happiness closes another opens, but often we look so long at the closed door that we do not see the one which has been opened before us."

Helen Keller

Wisdom of the Enneagram
By Don Richard Riso
and Russ Hudson

The Essential Rumi
Edited By Coleman Barks

Learning to Fly: Trapeze-Reflections on Fear, Trust, and the Joy of Letting Go
By Sam Keen

The Mozart Effect: Tapping the Power of Music to Heal the Body, Strengthen the Mind, and Unlock the Creative Spirit
By Don Campbell

Creating True Prosperity
By Shakti Gawain

Change Your Handwriting, Change Your Life
By Vimala Rodgers

Moxie Magazine www.moxiemag.com
"For the woman who dares"
510.540.5510

"One must be able to let things happen."
C. G. Jung

HEALINGS GONE WRONG

I WANTED TO WRITE ABOUT THE HEALINGS THAT DIDN'T WORK. THERE IS JUST AS MUCH TO LEARN FROM THOSE. BEING AN EXTREMIST, I TEND TO GO OVERBOARD AND TRY TO HURRY UP THE HEALING PROCESS, AND DO (MORE) OF WHATEVER IT IS.

I WILL SAY THAT MANY OF THE FOLLOWING TOOK PLACE A NUMBER OF YEARS AGO, AND I HAVE NOTICED THAT I AM MORE GENTLE WITH MY SELF-CARE.

Some examples:

I READ ABOUT HOW 10 MINUTES OF JUMPING ROPE EQUALS A MILE OR MORE OF RUNNING, SO I USED MY WILLPOWER TO JUMP FOR 20 MINUTES, EVEN THOUGH I WAS GASPING FOR AIR BY THE END OF IT. THE NEXT DAY I GOT UP AND COULDN'T WALK! MY CALF MUSCLES HAD TIGHTENED UP SO SEVERELY, I COULD ONLY HOP AROUND THE HOUSE. IT TOOK A FEW DAYS UNTIL I COULD WALK NORMALLY, AND I DON'T THINK I EVER JUMPED ROPE AGAIN.

I STARTED DRINKING SPIRULINA, WHICH IS A "GREEN WONDER DRINK" OF VITAMINS AND MINERALS FROM THE SEA. I DECIDED TO DO A 30-DAY FAST AND ONLY DRINK SPIRULINA.

It came in a powder that you mixed with water, and I remember gagging at the green globules as I tried to mix it.

By the third day, I hated the stuff, but my pride wouldn't let me admit it. I kept drinking glass after glass and saying I liked it.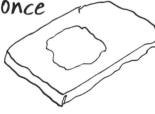

My younger brother still teases me about it.

Then I became convinced that I needed more iron in my diet and found the perfect natural remedy. You simmer applesauce in a cast-iron skillet, and the iron leaches out of the skillet, bonds with the applesauce, and becomes easily digestable. You are supposed to spread it on toast, one teaspoon once a day for several days but I misunderstood.

I ate a bowl of it. It turned my teeth black and made me nauseated for three days!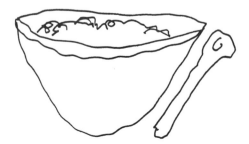

In my eagerness to heal, to become "better," I had actually injured, or made myself sick.

Here is a recent example of a "Healing Gone Wrong." I was having a massage on a cruise ship, and the therapist explained that she would be applying a gel to my back to "help remove toxins." I asked what was in the gel, and she said "peppermint, witch hazel, menthol, and aloe." This sounded great, so I gave my permission. As she spread the cool substance on my back, she said,

"You might feel a slight burning sensation."

I definitely felt a slight burning, which was rapidly increasing to a medium burning. She then laid a piece of crinkly paper on my back, which would be peeled off to reveal the new, toxin-free me.

Witch Hazel

crinkly paper to seal in the gel

She tore the paper off with a flourish, and now it was a Very Strong Burning sensation, and I yelled for her to get it all off of my back...   N o w !

She rushed for warm towels, and I began to cry.

The crying became sobbing and I laid there, chilled and still burning, gulping and hiccuping as I sobbed.

The massage therapist said,

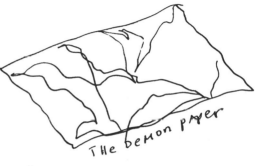
The demon paper

"I've never had anyone cry on my massage table. You must have a lot of toxins."

I rose up and looked right at her. "Listen. I've had an allergic reaction. The tears are normal. I DON'T have 'A lot of toxins' and I suggest you quickly show some sympathy."

She began chanting,

"Oh dear, oh dear, please don't tell my boss."

I finished crying and left the spa. In the old days, I would have been so embarrassed to cry, I would have hidden it or held it in, probably consoled the therapist, a_nd left a tip! I did none of these. (Well perhaps I consoled just a bit.)

Special note: I have hundreds of massages every year, and it is very rare to experience what I did.

We are entitled to speak up at the slightest sign of discomfort. We are allowed to be sensitive to "natural" materials and to have varying reactions to substances that have been used on thousands of others.

We can say, "No thank-you" and get up and leave at any point!

We don't need to participate in the toxin mentality: that there are bad things i_n us that we must get o_ut.

Our bodies are magnificently skilled instruments of recycling and change.

We can trust this.

98

Healing Stories

A woman told this story:

"When I was a little girl, I found a robin's egg and kept it in my room. Then I started peeling the shell because I got so excited to see what was in there. I kept peeling the shell even though my mom told me not to.

Well of course, I damaged the developing baby bird, and in doing this, it couldn't fully form." I realize that this is a metaphor for me now: As an adult I'm still forming and my picking at myself stunts and prevents my growth.

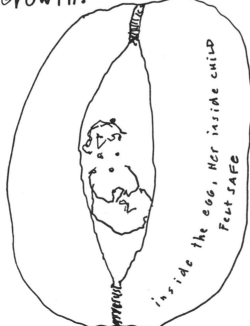

inside the egg, Her inside child Felt safe

So I made myself a giant egg to climb into! It has a zipper on the inside, and I spend time in there whenever I need to be made whole or given time to grow.

This is the story of the forlorn shoplifter and the laughing salespeople.

"She ripped off a bunch of stuff—I caught her by the arm—she doesn't speak English, the police are on their way."

This is what I heard when I walked into the store. The young woman they had caught sat dejectedly on a stool, twisting the strap of her purse and staring at the floor.

The salespeople laughed and smoked cigarettes and made fun of her clothes and stupidity. When I suggested they be more gentle, they said,

"Why? She doesn't even speak <u>English</u>."

All I could think of to do was draw a purple heart on a scrap of paper and hand it to her. She stared at it for an instant and then looked up with a disbelieving smile, nodded, and held up the tiny piece of paper.

My very dear Friend Ray rarely said
he loved me, And I noticed myself
Acting in ways I used to Act with
my father to try to find out if
he loved me. It was like Doing
emotional handstands or something
like that.

I HAD BECOME Quite GOOD
AT
eMotionAL AcroBAtics

On Valentine's Day, I called Ray to
talk to him About it. I wasn't even sure
what to say, and felt very uncertain
and insecure. Suddenly I Blurted out,

"Ray, Do you think you'd Be Able
to tell me you love me?"
There was A very long pause and
he said,
"Oh Susan. I'm so sorry I haven't
Been Able to say that I love you.
Because I Do, I really Do. I've
had difficulty expressing love All
my life. I Am so touched that
you Asked me this."

Our Friendship has changed and
deepened so much since that conversation.
I'm not going to wait anymore to
speak of love.

Ray recently made me this poster:

Hi Susan

I love you

Happy full moon. Summer

Ray

My neighbor across the street began
using a drill saw in the late afternoons.
It seemed like he timed it to interfere
with my nap time. I've discovered
that if I can find out something about
why the noise is happening, I am less
likely to despise it. So I went over
to introduce myself.

Hi Brad!

A sweet-faced man looked up from
his saw.

"Oh, I'm sorry, am I bothering you? Just
yell out your window and tell me to stop.
I'll go upstairs and read books or
something. I'm recovering from a
broken leg and making shelves that
my wife's asked for for 20 years."

We then discovered he had
serendipitously met my brother on the
ski slopes two years before! I met a
new neighbor and a friend.

My friend Patricia found this note
taped to a wall in a restaurant where she
was having breakfast and adjusting to
a recent move:

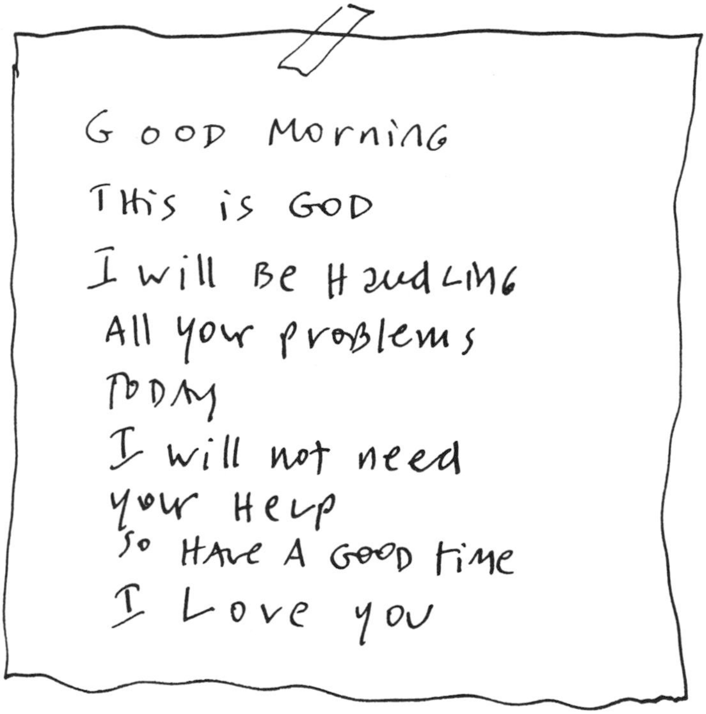

Good Morning

This is God

I will be handling
All your problems
Today
I will not need
your help
So have a good time
I Love you

I was listening to my inspiration
phone line, where people call in from
all over the world and leave marvelous
and inspiring messages. There was a
message from what sounded like four or five
people at work who had listened
to the message and then didn't
realize they were still being recorded.

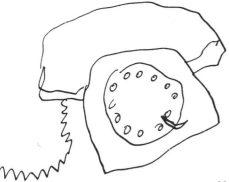

So they spoke candidly about SARK and I listened.

They said that I didn't really care about what I wrote, that I just wanted money, that I wasn't a very good writer or artist, that I was fatter than before...

I couldn't stop listening as they went on and on, speculating about everything in my life. It was compelling and horrifying, and a nightmare. I quickly erased the message and flung myself on my bed, sobbing. I felt angry and betrayed and so very I WAS SO HURT exposed. I wanted to speak to them and get revenge. I wanted to quit having an inspiration line.

After the tears, I called my brother Andrew. He listened to the whole terrible story and then asked if I wanted to hear a perspective that wasn't merely sympathetic.

I said I did.

"You've done this, what they did."

"Excuse me?" I said.

"You've discussed celebrities before. I've heard you. These people don't know you or your life. They're bored out of their minds at a job they probably don't like and you and your message were an easy target. You can't possibly take this personally and if you do, maybe you shouldn't have the phone line. Besides, why were you listening to them in the first place?"

I knew that everything he said was true, and after some more tears and emotional process work, it began to be funny to me. Now I hold no grudges and forgive these people. I also pay a lot more attention to what I say about other people, recorded or not.

well, maybe a tiny grudge...

I forgive

Also, I no longer listen to people who don't know they're still being recorded!

After my last love relationship ended,
I began compiling a list of things I
wouldn't tolerate in another relationship.
This list included:

> - Must not snore
> - Be actively engaged
>   in psychological work
> - Be physically active
> - not travel extensively

Then I realized, what would I
tolerate in another relationship? or would
my list of intolerances just grow longer
and longer? As I made a list of what
I would tolerate, I realized I was
just listing my own faults!

That night, I had a dream where
the contents of my "list" became clear.

> any and all faults
> welcome as long as
> person is consciously
> aware and in process
> of working on them

During the development of my meditation practice, I began to want the image of Buddha nearby. So I started shopping for Buddha statues and none of them seemed right.
One day, I sat down in a store with one I was considering buying, and jumped up to say,

The possibly mocking Buddha

"This Buddha is mocking me!"
    It greatly amused me to hear the shop person reply,
    "Oh no, Buddha doesn't mock!"
    I finally found a sweet faced, nonmocking Budd<u>ha</u>!

My sweet faced Buddha

Actually, it's even sweeter faced than this. The pen was mocking me!

P.S. I think Buddha added HA! to the name for added humor.

Eleven years ago, I rented and moved into what I call "The Magic Cottage," which is a 180-square-foot former toolshed. At the time I moved in, I had a dollar in the bank.

1 Cottage
1 Dollar

Last year, the cottage, garden, and apartment building were put up for sale, for a lot more than one dollar.

When I heard that the Magic Cottage was going to be sold, I was very concerned about many things, including the garden, which was very overgrown and very special to me.

The Secret Garden

The property manager called to say that the garden needed to be cut down to show the property lines. She did allow me to pay half so I could choose people with some sensitivity and heart.

Still, on the day scheduled, I cried
and clung to all the vines and leaves
I'd looked at for 11 years. The gardeners
were very kind and reassuring to me,
and one of them said,

"The brittle branches need to be
cut back so that other things can grow.
The flexible ones can stay."

I decided that this was a metaphor
for life. Now, a year later, I see
the garden overgrown once again.

The flexible ones can stay...

As it turned out, the owner put
the property on the market and
people came to open houses and
began bidding on the property.

read the poem
The Guesthouse
By Rumi

I started raising money and
hired a Realtor and Mortgage Broker.

Bless Him   Thank you miracle worker

I made offers, which were turned
down. Finally, I gave up.

I went on retreat and prayed
for guidance. My friend Robyn asked,
        "What does the smallest part
            of you want to do?"
    I instantly replied,
        "I want to stay."

At that instant, an 80-foot-tall warrior woman rose up in me and said, SHOUTED

"I will Buy the Property!"

I came home and said to my Realtor,

"I know how to make the next offer... with humility."

He joked, "What's that?"

"No time deadlines, a heartfelt note from me, and every penny I can muster."

Money came from my company, my Mother and Brother, my Friends who own a restaurant, and from a new Book deal.

The owner said yes the same Day, and turned down a matching offer that would have made her more money. Thank you Nancy

She was part
Warrior
Viking
Angel
Nurse
Nurturing parent
Protector
Defender
She came to Help me

It was a true Miracle and taught me a lot about intention and manifestation.

I learned to direct my energy and work fully on my own Behalf, even if it seemed crazy or unreasonable to others. I learned to allow spirit to work through me, without attachment to the result. I also learned that giving up is not always the end of the story.

THE HEALING STORIES SURROUND US

All of our stories Are VALUABLE and HAVE HEALING POTENTIAL

Kids too!

There Are lessons to Be learned everywHere if we will let Go of Being Angry victims, passive OBservers, or rigHteous resistant rebels, just to name A few personas.

I Am Astonished By the Amount and quality of love that is Available if we will Ask and participate and show up for

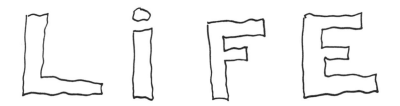

LiFE

I Hope that you share and Circulate your own Healing stories. We need them.

PATRICIA
and BRANDY

Some of the most extraordinary connections in our lives happen in the most ordinary ways.

I had a sore neck, and was asking at a metaphysical bookstore for a massage therapist. Ginna referred me to Patricia, and I drove to her home office.

An ebullient woman holding a tiny dog answered the door and ushered me in. She immediately handed me the dog, which fastened itself to my clothes like a small brooch. This small dog was emanating a most powerful aura, and Patricia was swirling around, asking me curious and pointed questions about my health. I began to realize that this would be more than a neck massage. Much more.

She gave me herbal and homeopathic remedies and led me into her treatment room. (radiant things were happening...)

What transpired in that room really deserves a book of its own, yet here is a glimpse:

As I lay face down on her table, Patricia began an extraordinary energy healing/intuitive medicine session that included: visualizing, magnet therapy, physical therapy, and psychology. I felt like Dorothy in The Wizard of Oz when she goes to get fixed up before meeting the Wizard.

In fact, Patricia's laugh reminded me of Glenda, the Good Witch!

I learned an astonishing amount about my body and energy systems, and psychological makeup. It felt very deep, easy, and profound and I knew I would be returning here often for many more healing sessions. Brandy is an amazing component in the whole healing process. He affixed himself to different parts of my body that needed healing.

Patricia has been working in the healing realms for many years as an RN and physical therapist, as well as other traditions. She describes a near-death experience that sent her back with many more healing gifts.

Brandy fastened to the front of me like a small brooch

I am so very blessed to receive her work as a healer, mentor, and coach. She illuminates my life and I honor her voluminous contributions to my healing journey and to this book. (She also works well by phone)

Patricia Huntington is a registered holistic health care practitioner, mentor, and intuitive counselor. She specializes in homeopathic therapies and transformational process.

Patricia can be reached at:
P.O. Box 22132
Carmel, CA 93922
By phone at (831) 625-5177
on Tuesdays from 8 A.M.—7 P.M. PST

SARK peers out from behind Brandy

Rebecca Latimer

I discovered a book called <u>You're Not Old Until You're Ninety</u>...<u>Best to Be Prepared</u>, however. I thought it would be interesting to read about life from the perspective of a 94-year-old.

I had no idea how fascinating and remarkable this book would be, and how much I would learn from it. The book includes her psychological, psychic, and telepathic explorations, and speaks about some of my mentors: Alan Watts, Paul Reps, Ram Dass. It also introduced me to new and illuminating characters. I learned about cultivating my own inner doctor(s) and new thoughts about dying. It is tempting to write on and on about this book!

I went to meet Rebecca when she gave a reading and book signing. Her presence is feisty and warm, sharp and deep. I knew we would become friends.

As a suggested experiment, I stood on top of a chair at the book signing for 10 minutes. Very interesting!

Rebecca traveled the world for 25 years with her husband, who was an officer in the foreign service. Rebecca's own work was essentially censored during that time, and she is working on a new book called Autobiography of an Unconscious Feminist.

Rebecca says, "Remember, it's your body that's aging, not you! I'd rather be over 70 than under 50."

When I told her I was 45, she declared, "Oh good. Now some real work can begin."

Rebecca is a marvelous role model for "doing it anyway," despite fear or lack of knowledge. She tells people,

"Don't worry about how it's done. You don't have to actually do it well to have a good effect!"

We write and phone each other, and I visit for tea, but surely our deepest connection is in the telepathic and spirit worlds. I love Rebecca!

Lucky news:
Rebecca's journals, letters, manuscripts, and other papers have all been reserved for future housing in the permanent "Rebecca Latimer Special Collection" at Mills College Library in Oakland, California.

BIBBO

"Dancing with the Crown Chakra"

My friend Brigette kept saying, "Someday you must have a haircut by Bibbo. He's amazing."

Since I already had my hair cut by my very dear Cecilia, I didn't see any need to experiment with this odd-sounding person. Yet Brigette beamed whenever she spoke of him. Then Cecilia took some time off, and I went to Bibbo.   it's like a new land

Bibbo lives in love and light and shines it on everyone. I had a haircut, an effortless, lovely haircut, and as excellent as it was, it was almost incidental to the love I experienced there. I left feeling taller, younger, and more beautiful in my own soul.

Bibbo dances around, laughing and bestowing blessings on every person who comes near. It is genuine and clearly from his soul. He is one of those people who feeds spirits with his essence.

My intuition also tells me that he is grounded, very spiritual, and based deeply in his family. I marvel at the spirit of Bibbo and his "hair healings."

Thank you Brigette, CeciliA, Judy, silvana!

BIBBO HAIR SALON   260 POST ST SF CA   415.421.2426

Gordon MacKenzie

There is A marvelous book called Orbiting the Giant Hairball written by A highly creative imp, A spiritual shaman, and extremely original thinker named Gordon Mackenzie.

I went to meet him when he came to San Francisco For A book signing. The picture on the back of his book was very tiny, and I didn't know exactly what he looked like, so when I saw an older gentleman in A brown leather jacket browsing through books, I thought it was him. But wait! This man was dry and cracked and appeared quite crabby. This couldn't be Gordon MacKenzie!

It wasn't. Gordon stepped From behind A pillar where he was attaching A clothesline for his presentation and instantly said,
"Oh my dear SARK" As though he'd known me forever.

I said something about having dinner together afterward and his response was an immediate and delighted,
"Yes, of course!"   He had color-full suspenders

There was a small assortment of people there that night, and Gordon treated them royally and with infinite respect. He began with odd parts of drawings clipped to a clothesline and then asked people to point out the one that spoke most to them. The first drawing chosen was of a chicken, and he revealed that his father hypnotized chickens! I nearly jumped out of my chair because my mother had hypnotized chickens! The evening was full of such serendipitous gems.

His | work | and Life | were Genius

Gordon worked at Hallmark Cards for 30 years and writes gorgeously of the creative process and what it needs to thrive. We went on to dinner and a conversation of the ages. true magic Just before Gordon's death, his dear wife, Louise, helped me speak to him by phone and his elegant voice answered my tears and questions. When I told him he would be in this book, he said,
"Oh, my dear. That would be lovely."
Yes, Gordon, you are lovely.

Donna Eden

This marvelous soul, energy worker, and healer gave a workshop that I attended. We met when she called for a woman wearing an underwire bra to come up on stage.

She fluttered the energy at the lymph

I was wearing an underwire bra!

points beneath my breasts and then muscle-tested me. I lost all energy instantly. She then manipulated my spleen points and they were so sensitive, I almost lept through the ceiling. I no longer wear underwire bras and work with my spleen and lymph points daily.

Donna has been doing energy healing work on herself and for others for 25 years. Together with her husband, David, she wrote <u>Energy Medicine</u>.

She travels and teaches throughout the world. Her book and videos are enormously helpful and full of simple, clear ways to feel healthier and more energetic every day. I use these methods daily. I am amazed at how much there is to learn about energy. I am keenly interested in anything that allows me to expand upon and multiply my energy. I know that these are the systems we need to learn to magnify good health.

Donna Eden and her work are such a valuable addition to our community of healing.

To find out more about Donna, to order her book, or for her workshop schedule, call

(541) 482-1800, ext. 2   or   www.innersource.net

Tori

I first met Tori, my massage therapist, at Ventana in Big Sur, by a fragrant, wood-burning fireplace. I soon realized that this was way beyond massage, and in fact was an energetic healing experience of great presence and love.

We laughed in recognition, and a friendship has grown beautifully over the years.

Tori reminds me of a heliotrope, of pussy willows, and of the ancestor grandmothers sitting in healing circles, in nature camps, when all healing traditions were a way of life.

She is a healer, a divine spirit and visionary with gifts of energy, heart space, and the arts of being human.

I consider her one of my mentors of excellent health. She lived in Big Sur for many years, and is still surrounded by the mystery and strength of that place. Nature anchors Tori, and she seeks out magnificent dwellings in this world to call home.

I am reminded of the great feminine when I see Tori, and since we are both highly sensitive beings, we often communicate in long, emotion-filled voice mail messages. Tori's presence on this earth is a gift to us all whether you physically meet her or not.

To contact Tori about Living Aloha Retreats, email her at: livingaloha@mailco-op.com

Robyn Posin

Robyn tenderly and majestically does her essence-supporting healing work from her tent and hammock and wild places in Ojai, California.

I deeply trust people who have stopped "doing" and turned intently toward their Being self. Robyn shares this Being with the world.

I first read her Affirmation Cards, "For the little ones inside," and called the number on the back. Serendipitously, I found myself speaking with Robyn. She ended our mirthful and illuminating conversation by saying, "Would you prefer to be the initiator of our next communication?" This thoughtful sentence drew me to contact her again, and over the years we have become phonic, telepathic, and in-person friends. I quote her on my inspiration phone line and am thrilled to introduce you to her. If her work resonates with you, do reach toward her.

Robyn L. Posin, Ph.D.
P.O. Box 725
Ojai, CA 93024

You Are Never:

Too Sensitive
Too Serious
Too Particular
Too _____

What You May Be Is:

More Sensitive
More Serious
More Particular
More _____

Than The People You're Around Feel Comfortable With...

Consider Not Being With Them At Such Times!

805.646.4518 or www.forthelittleonesinside.com

The Fool

Joshua Kadison

Joshua is a maker of healing music, creator of the book <u>Seventeen Ways to Eat A Mango</u>, and deep lover of life.

I was priveleged to listen to him play and sing his "story songs" on a ranch in Santa Barbara, with candles tipping and tilting, and curtains blowing in the night air.

We became friends, and our friendship feels like the kind that emerges from childhood, where you collect marbles together and pore over pages of beloved books.   I think he is a wood elf.

One time he flew up from Santa Barbara for the day to take me to lunch. He arrived in a white convertible and announced his arrival at my house by playing the flute. Later, we became impossibly lost in the car, in the rain, and laughed until we could barely drive. I think of Joshua as a tarot card come to life. He enriches my life, and those of so many others, every day.

For more information about Joshua, check his web site at www.joshuakadison.com

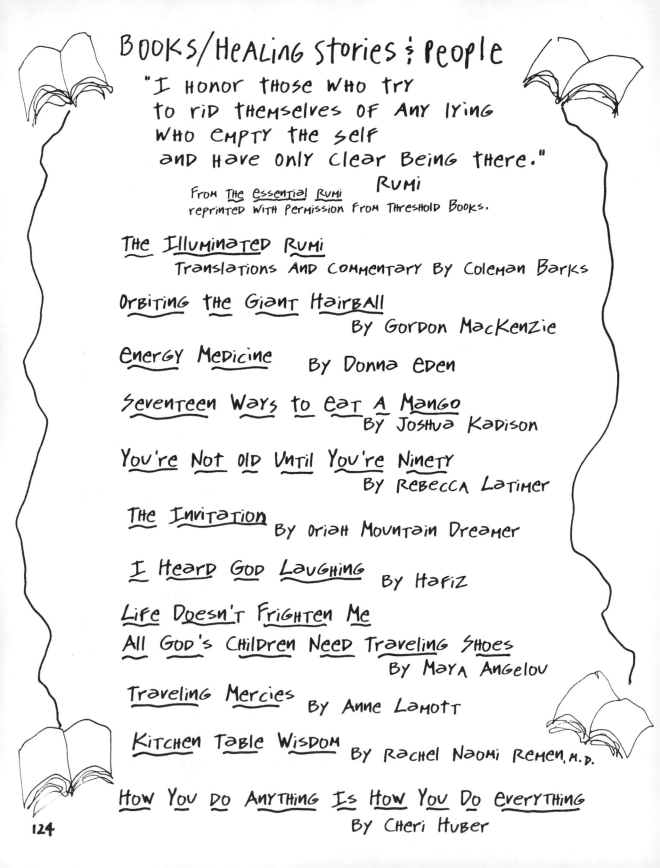

Books/Healing Stories & People

"I honor those who try
to rid themselves of any lying
who empty the self
and have only clear being there."
                    Rumi

From The Essential Rumi
reprinted with permission from Threshold Books.

The Illuminated Rumi
        Translations and Commentary by Coleman Barks

Orbiting the Giant Hairball
                    By Gordon MacKenzie

Energy Medicine   By Donna Eden

Seventeen Ways to Eat a Mango
                    By Joshua Kadison

You're Not Old Until You're Ninety
                    By Rebecca Latimer

The Invitation   By Oriah Mountain Dreamer

I Heard God Laughing   By Hafiz

Life Doesn't Frighten Me
All God's Children Need Traveling Shoes
                    By Maya Angelou

Traveling Mercies   By Anne Lamott

Kitchen Table Wisdom   By Rachel Naomi Remen, M.D.

How You Do Anything Is How You Do Everything
                    By Cheri Huber

WHAT I'M WORKING ON

it helps to remember and be reminded that we are all working in the soup together

We forget constantly that we are not alone. I share these notes as reminders that we are all SPECTACULARLY FLAWED, splendidly imperfect, and often misguided.

The Buddhist meditation teacher Pema Chödrön, in response to someone asking why we continually forget, says:

"We forget and remember, forget and remember. That's why it's called practice."

And so we must practice every day and retrain our minds and hearts, and most importantly, be present for whatever it is.

There is a marvelous quote that says "if we're supposed to learn from our mistakes, then we must need to make a lot of them."

Here are some of the places in my own soul I'm struggling with, noticing, or being with.

I had Been Stung By Criticism of my Artwork. one Critic Said,

"These Books Are A real Mess."

So, MY OWN inner Critics Picked Up their Weapons And Shouted:

"I'M So Sick of Your Constipated Scandinavian Designs!"

"Anyone's Art is Better or More Adventurous than Yours!"

"You are So Scared to experiment With Anything new!"

inner Critics love To Speak With Underlines And exclamation Points

This Was During A time When All I Could Do Was Wake Up And eat Fritos.

Then I had to Complete And turn in More Art.Work.

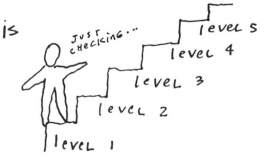

People Say to Me,

"But you've Done All this therapy, have A Healer, A Company, But YOU Are A

Bestselling Author

How Hard Can it Be?"

What they're really Saying is that they Hope the Pain ends When they Get to A Certain level.

it Doesn't.

level 5
level 4
level 3
level 2
level 1

JUST cHecking...

Let's just all realize and admit that the pain never ends and go on brilliantly anyway.

*Brilliantly, in this case, means: Despite all forms of wanting to quit

Let's realize that to experience our lives intimately means to be off-balance, out of control, and subject to all sorts of fragile and tender emotions.

We might say, "Then why do it?"

"Why not hide, avoid, resist, anesthetize, refuse, neglect, lie, work harder, gain more control, get more money, seek more escapes, and live in denial?"

You'll do all of these anyway

And the pain just waits for another entry point.

Pain waited for entry

The real and indelible blessing is that to be truly present in our own lives also means that we're there for all the ecstasy and joy, as well as all the pain.   Pain heals

Oh, that! Joy is tougher to accept than pain. Isn't this a curious paradox. We are often more comfortable with pain and struggle because it's familiar.

There is a book in my house called <u>How Much Joy Can You Stand</u>? By Suzanne Falter-Barns. When people come over to visit, they often pick up that book and comment on how that title awakens something in them. I believe that we are so unaccustomed to living in joy that we actually create suffering and wrap it like a familiar cloak around ourselves. We forget that it is our right and privilege to live in a state of joy. Be willing to notice just how much joy you're creating and living with.

we can hang up our cloaks of suffering

Person Bounces in an Orb of Joy

reminder note: a state of joy is very different from mindless positivity...

"The trick is not how much pain you feel but how much joy you feel."   Erica Jong

"You will deeply feel that the greater your ecstasy, your pleasure, and your joy, the more you contribute to the world."   William Reich

I am in the process of healing the following: (later I will list tools for change and acceptance.)

• Addiction to suffering, overreacting, complimenting myself with euphoria, detriment seeking with self-loathing, leaping to conclusions, and highly emotional states of being

128

- Relentlessly seeking input:
    Phone Messages, compliments,
    recognition, credit, Drama

Fear of
- Allowing others to witness my pain or vulnerability

- Admitting that something/someone hurt me

- Carrying image of myself as utterly important
  and unchanging

- Perfectionism and the following shame

- Not taking responsibility for my projections

- Not feeling all the feelings as they occur

- Avoiding meditation   NOT NOW...

I have healed, and am in process of healing:
- My secret binge eating

- Not living healthily in my physical body

- Not having objectivity in my emotional responses

- Not being fully present in my own life

- Having no "Adult" present, and being run
  by subpersonalities or upset inner children

- Allowing my inner critics to work against me

- Not trusting my self/life   EXIT

I still look for the exits, for the fastest
way. I try to outrun my neurosis, move
to turn off whatever I find unpleasant, or

129

ADJUST FOR COMFORT.

I AM specific and definite, and also sometimes harsh in my expressions.

sometimes people get scared of me! eek

I AM practicing loving-kindness and cultivating gentleness. I AM working on my tendency to be easily irritated and trying to control others and the environment.

I CAN sit with pain now. Pain

I AM learning to accept my flaws and live side by side with them. I've developed an aware ego and can disengage from narcissism.   At times...

There is so much healing still to do, and I CAN trust in the process of life to bring me all the lessons and teachers! Thank you Teachers

Of course, I still cringe as I re-read what I have written here.

Person learns to stand in acceptance

I'D rather not Admit All these things, yet
I know that the secrecy and shame makes
A Greenhouse For All of it to Grow larger and
thicker.

The
GreenHouse
of
FLaws

We Can share our Abundant Flaws and laugh
At HOW similar We All Are.

I Am no longer Ashamed to Be Human!

We Can Fart exuberantly together and
laugh until We Feel ill. We Can talk
All night About everything and nothing — we
Can welcome each other's tears, and
wildly Celebrate our Joys and successes.

Let's take All our masks off and
see the soft, teary, wistful Face that
lives underneath.

All the masks Flew OFF and
revealed SAD and truthFul FACes

I'm still trying to perform for love.
"Maybe if I did..." "Maybe if I said..."
"Maybe if I was...., _____ would
love me more, better, longer, deeper."

My younger brother, Andrew, pointed this
out in a very poignant way. I had lifted
up the flap of this belief system by
admitting that I thought if I showed
up to support him on a special day, it
would mean that he would love me
more. He looked at me with tears in
his eyes and said,

"Oh Susan. How could you ever think
I could love you _any_ _more_ than I already do?"

Then we both cried.

This way of experiencing love conditionally
has its roots in my earlier days.

The roots were old and anciently placed. excavation!

I am easing these roots out of the ground
and giving them new places to grow

132

I AM now learning to (receive love) As
well As Give it. I thought the receiving
WAS AUTOMATIC, and Discovered that
it's More OF A Process than that.
The Ability to receive love CAN Be Blocked
Or Distorted By earlier woundings, or
experiences of loss and Betrayal.

We CAN learn new WAYs and experiences
OF receiving love As we witness ourselves
Turn AWAY From love. The WOUNDING CAN
teach Us where love needs to enter.

Holes in Her where love Blew through

All PATCHED UP so (love) can Hang out inside

More Tears Please

◊ We Are Afraid to Cry.

◊ We Are Afraid to Be seen As Weak, or Falling Apart, or not (Fun!) to Be With.

◊ We Cry, and then Apologize. We only Cry in Front of Certain People. We only Cry When We're Alone, or We Can't Cry.

Crying is not spoken of enough.

When Princess Diana Was killed, the images and sounds of so many people crying together really touched me.

All kinds of people cried together

I make my inspiration phone line messages with the prayer that people will feel free to cry, and many do. Some people just call up and cry.

Sometimes people say, "I know you think tears Are inspiring, But it's Hard to let go."

lines of tears

inspiration phone Line   415·546·3742
24 Hours

We must let go and

TUMBLe

Through our interiors with no handholds, and fall limply down, our clothes damp from tears.

We must cry together, and hold each other As our shoulders shake.

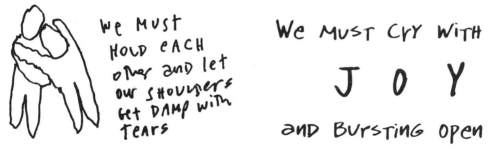

We must hold each other and let our shoulders get damp with tears

We must cry with

J O Y

and bursting open

At the stunning beauty and kindness in this world. SO MUCH BEAUTY

We must cry when we encounter our primitive loneliness and wake up gasping at 4 A.M.

Cry More often

We must cry at the injustices and evil and violence in our world.

Cry Again

I think that until we cry as often
as we laugh, we are not fully alive.

Cry For No reason

Our tears are the waterfall of the
soul and it is _our right_ to experience
and express sadness and other feelings
through tears.

Don't Block Tears

When you feel that distinctive tingle behind your eyes, let the tears out

Your tears live inside of you and want
to flow freely.

No More Apologies For Tears!

I welcome your tears and encourage
my own.

Let's cry together when we meet.

esalen

In Big Sur, California, there is a spiritual community, teaching place, and sacred land called esalen, named after the Native American tribe called the esselen.

It balances on the edge of land overlooking the Pacific Ocean, and is blessed with natural hot springs and the stunning beauty of the land of Big Sur.

I have visited many times over the years and stayed in the simple rooms and eaten the spectacular food. I've sat in the gardens at full moon and swam naked in the pool. I've sat in meditation and played & napped in the art barn. I've admired the gazebo school for kids, and have gotten lost on trails near the property.

I've cried in the hot springs, and laughed during massages with Pacific sea spray on my back. I've fought with friends, hidden from Gestalt Therapy sessions, argued with people at the front gate, hated the rules of the place, and adored so many moments at esalen.

esalen institute
Highway One
Big Sur CA 93920
(831) 667·3000 (catalog requests + general information)

TASSAJARA
Zen Mountain Center

AT THE END of A long, BUMPY, DUSty, UnPAVED ROAD is TASSAJARA. It is A spiritual community of MEDITAtORS AND seekers, with NATURAL HOT SpRiNGS, rAttlesnAKES, AND PATHS Lit By lanterns AT NIGHT. It is Also A PlACE of GrEAT NATURAL BEAUty. it is HIGH in the MOUNTAINS ABOVE BIG SUR

I'D BEEN invited to Go for yEARS AND HAD RESISTED BECAUSE of VARiOUS FEARS: DiscomFort, PlaNNiNG in ADVANCE, AND of BEING FORCED or COERCEd to MEDITATE. THis is HilARiOUS, SinCE the Art of MEDITATIon DoESNt RESPOND to pressure, AND Zen DoESNt ADVOCATE coercion. Still, Me AND MY Little FEARS went to TASSAJARA THiS SUMMER AND HAD A spleNDid TIME. I will return TO TASSAJARA.

I HID OUT in the little liBrARy in The woods UP in The loFT AND PEERED in AT the DHARMA TALKS. I SOAKED in the sulphur spRiNGS, AND lAid in the river NAKED. I sHUFFLED ArouND in MY PAJAMAS AND DRANK MANY MUGS of LApSANG SOUCHONG teA. with cream I SAT in the outDoor Hot POOL AND WATCHED SHootiNG STARS. I AM SURE I HEARD GOD LAUGHING THAT NIGHT.

We MUST support spiritual teAching Here Are A Few NEARBY HARBIN/CA OMEGA/ n.y. HollyHOCK/ B.c. BreitenBUSH oregon

AND NURTURE Communities Henry Miller library CA. FiNDHORN/Scotland SHENOA/CA. GAMPO ABBEY/ NOVA SCOTIA

TASSAJARA: 300 PAGE Street
San Francisco CA
94102
415. 863. 3136
(Closed LABor DAy — MAY 1st)

Trees

I've written often of my love for Trees, and for hugging them. (Close your eyes and you wont feel as self-conscious.) Now I've taken to complimenting them verbally. I have Tree friends in my neighborhood that I stop and speak to, and admire out loud.

I dream about the roots of trees and where they travel underneath us, and how they sustain us from above. I marvel at tree canopies and spectacular branches. I see how trees bring people together, in saving or sustaining their existence and growth.

The healing powers of trees are surrounding us every day. They quietly stand in loving presence, and are so intrinsic to our good health that we forget their magnificence and their place in our healing lives.

Pay tribute
to a tree
today
and make it
a visible prayer
in your
life

"What lovely branches you have."

in honor of my godchild Zoe age 5 who climbed her first tree with me, Sept. 1999 Tree climbing bliss...

140

Gardens

My friend Elissa told me that one night she was digging in her garden, and deep in the cool soil she uncovered glowing green glints in the earth.

Emerald night treasures!

Elissa is sustained and healed by the act of gardening.

My friend Isabel has a garden we visit like a dear friend for tea.

The people at Findhorn, a spiritual community in Scotland, tell incandescent stories of their gardens and what grows there,

MY GARDEN IS A WILD PLACE THAT I WATCH.

My friend Brigette grows things on her fire escape and back stairs. One day she will have a beach cottage in the midst of blooming flowers.

Our gardens grow and swell like our hearts do. Gardens connect humans to the earth and heal disconnected places. Gardens are beautiful healing places that renew us. We can witness all of life's cycles in our gardens.

I know that F A i r i e s live, play, and dance in our gardens.

I know this.

OUR HEALING BEDS

THE land of counterpane

I FOLD into my mattress sometimes, A dive from some great height, A disappearance from worldly matters. I do a lot of HEALING in Bed and in DREAMS.

Beds Are our ADULT CRADLES. We need soft respite from our stumbling and striving. A bed is A SACRED land, A SHeltered territory, And A place to rebuild ourselves. As my Friend Robert used to say,

"May I have A Bit of Blanket and place to lie down?"

This is often All we need For HEALING.

I used to MAKE my BED ÷ I Don't anymore. It seems easier to get into and out of more often. Beds Are truly HEALING places that support much more than merely sleeping. We could say,

"GOOD night, I'm Going to my HEALING place now..."

S L e e p D e A r H e A r T

BOOKS / HOLY PLACES

"Between the conscious and
the unconscious, the mind has
put up a swing: All earth creatures,
even the supernovas, sway between
these two trees."
                                    Kabir

Faith in the Valley   By Iyanla Vanzant

Sabbath: Restoring the Sacred Rhythm of Rest
                                    By Wayne Muller

A Room of Her Own: Women's Personal Spaces
                                    By Chris Casson Madden

Kite Strings of the Southern Cross:
    A Woman's Travel Odyssey   By Laurie Gough

Awakening the Buddha Within   By Lama Surya Das

Tracks   By Robyn Davidson

My Family and Other Animals
                                    By Gerald Durrell

Paradise Found   By Stanley Young
                                    Photographs By Melba Levick

Pilgrim at Tinker Creek   By Annie Dillard

"The clamorous owl that nightly hoots
and wonders at our quaint spirits."
    From a sculpture by Leonard Baskin
            at Smith College

HeALinG School CurriculuM

I WAS one of those "KiDS WiTH PoTeNTiAL"
(AS All KiDS Are!) WHO WAS FrusTrATeD By THe
reGimeNTeD SYSTeM of eDuCATion I Grew up WiTH.
I loNGeD For A CreATive, HeAliNG School experience
AnD ofTeN DreAmeD of WHAT THe "ClASSeS" WOulD
CONSiST OF. Here is MY PArTiAl liST:

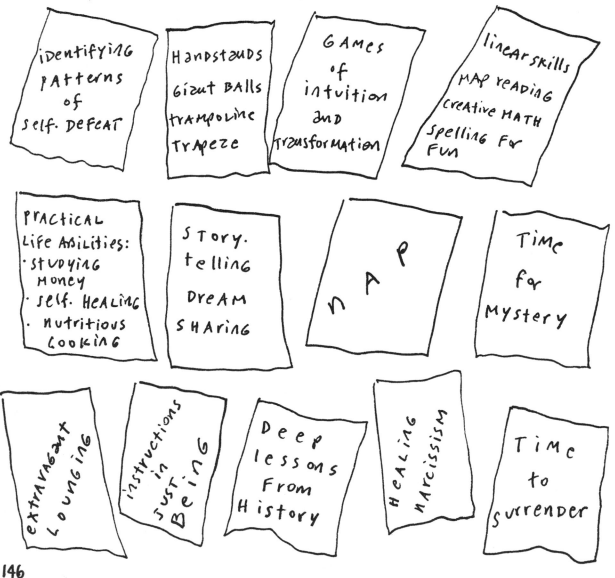

IDeNTifYiNG
PATTerns
of
Self. DefeAT

HandsTauDS
GiAnT BAlls
TrAMPoLiNe
TrApeze

GAMes
of
intuition
and
TrAnsforMation

liNeAr Skills
MAP reADiNG
CreATive MATH
SPelliNG For
FuN

PrACTiCAl
Life ABiLiTies:
· STvDYiNG
  Money
· Self. HeALiNG
· NuTritious
  CookiNG

STory.
TelliNG
DreAM
SHAriNG

n A P

Time
for
MYSTerY

exTrAvAGAnT
LounGing

instructions
in
JuST
BeiNG

Deep
lessons
From
HisTory

HeALiNG
NArcissism

Time
to
SurreNDer

self-esteem
meditation
stretching

congratulations
Prosperity

inventions

SOCIAL
JUSTICE
FIELD
DAYS

Dance
Drums
Design

Pleasure
reADing

MirAcle
WALKS
and
ADventures

lessons
of the
inner
critics

learning
to
invest
in
your self

Transpersonal
THerApy
Life
COACHing

How to Be
of
Service
to
others

Accepting
success

recycling
of
MATeriALS
creAtive
re·use

DAYs
Doing
noThing

visiting
HeAlers
inspiring
visitors

Sleeping
For
entertainment

Serendipity
synchroncity
randomness

eMotionAl
and
FeeLings
identification

permission
Slips
for
ecstasy

Gifts
of
procrastination

interspecies telepathic communication

non-competitive play and exercise for no result

SEXUAL HEALING VIBRATORS Tantra

ADMITTING our Genius

PARTICIPATING without MEASURING PROGRESS + DOING WHAT WE'RE not GOOD AT

Allowing and resolving conflict

Total self-love MARRYING THE self

PARENTING PRACTICE and Tests

ABUNDANCE in All FORMS

GRATITUDE and HUMILITY

In MY SCHOOL MODEL, DAYS AND NIGHTS WOULD Be so lively and REWARDING THAT a three-DAY WEEKEND WOULD naturally Be Chosen. School WOULD START AT DIFFERENT times OF THE DAY AND NIGHT to ALLOW FOR Alternative sleep schedules.

I Believe THAT THERE IS MUCH to Heal AND Change in OUR Current educational SYSTEM. We MUST All Care deeply THAT Arts Are Being removed From Public schools And WORK to Find new FUNDING SYSTEMS to replace THEM.

CASH Money $$

We MUST FIND More and new VEHICLES

WITH MONEY for ARTS EDUCATION

Here is my DREAM newspaper HEADLINE
For the present:

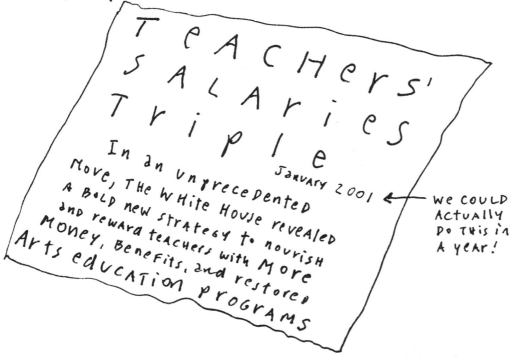

TEACHERs'
SALARIES
Triple
January 2001

In an unprecedented
move, The White House revealed
a bold new strategy to nourish
and reward teachers with more
money, benefits, and restored
Arts education programs

WE COULD
ACTUALLY
DO THIS in
A YEAR!

I wonder why sports Are so revered, And
schools so underfunded. We need to change
our Beliefs About the value of education And

illuminate our
wealth in Growing souls

As the light reached
THEM, Growing souls
popped up and
Blossomed

Faith

When you walk to the edge of all the light you have
and take that first step into the darkness of the unknown
you must believe that one of two things will happen:

There will be something solid for you to stand upon,
or, you will be taught how to fly

Patrick Overton

Secret Heart

The secret is
not in your
hand
or your
eye
or your
voice,
My aunt once
told me. The
secret is in
your heart.
Of course, she said, knowing
that doesn't make it any easier.

By Brian Andreas

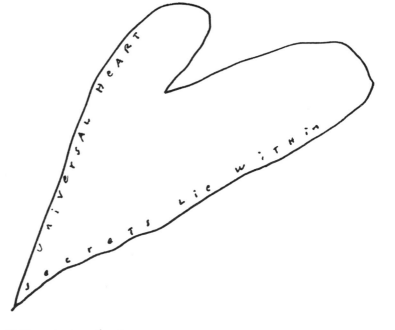

Healing Time in our Lives

Clock of your Life

. . . . What do the words
on your clock of
life say?

Fill in words instead of numbers
of how you would like to be living life

Sometimes I experience something I call
"The tyranny of a beautiful day." It can
feel like a weight or a pressure to "get
out and enjoy it!" "Do something fun!"
Sometimes I'm in a stormy mood on a
beautiful day and just want to stay inside.
I've learned to bring the beautiful day
inside and not feel compelled to go out.

Sometimes I feel tyrannized by plans.
is there a tyranny theme here?

I want them, yet I often dread doing
whatever it is when the time comes. I
finally figured out that what I want is
flexible plans that grow or change
according to my energy and mood (and
the other person's).

151

Flexible Plans Allow For Changes in time and location or Activity. Checking in with the other Person and Asking For A true read on energy and mood Can lead to Fabulous new Plans Born of the Present Moment, and not the Previous Plan.

Cancelling A Plan Can Be the most self-relieving, nurturing thing to do. It's especially sweet when it turns into A spontaneous nap.

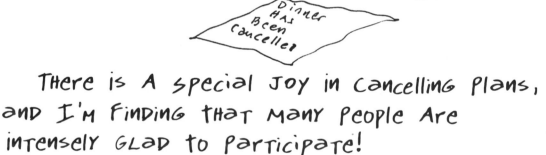

FABulous new Plans!

Solo luxury Date

SHARED DREAM circle

TRAVEL to ZANZIBAR

Dinner Has Been Cancelled

There is A special Joy in Cancelling Plans, and I'm Finding that many people Are intensely Glad to Participate!

Our Plans need to nourish and Support us. Plans Born of obligation Are often tinged with martyrdom or an Attempt to "Get more love." Yet real Friends Don't Keep Score, they Don't Care who invited who to what and when.

Or who called who!

Of course, there are times we are needed to make a plan to assist someone in a life event. Even then, we can make real plans that support our true nature.

My brother Andrew will help someone move, but he draws the line at the box packing part. He'll be the box-moving guy, but he's learned that he despises the packing part.

I will help someone move by taking him or her out for dinner and providing moral support and gifts. I've also loaned money to pay professional movers. I've also learned that I'm happy to pick people up from the airport if it's at night.

If people would tell the truth about what they're truly willing to do, there would be room for us all to help each other in many more ways.

Our time and energy are precious and need to be spent consciously.

Vicarious Activity is one of my favorite types of plans. It involves me staying home and mentally traveling along to whatever event it is and then hearing the details later. Telepathy works nicely in this way also.

I also use something I call

Time Stretcher — Time Shrinker

for various activities that call for one or both of these states. If I have a lot of work to do, am overwhelmed, and can't imagine-how-it-will-all-get-done, I call for the energy of the time stretcher. (Just ask for it to appear.)

I've experienced true miracles of time telescoping down and hands of the clock moving microscopically slow.

Time stretcher pulls time sideways and makes more space

Time Shrinker works when in traffic, or doing something tedious and repetitive and you want time to speed up!

There is an acronym I invented, which is P. U. S. :

Pressure
Urgency
Scarcity

I try to do nothing that originates from one of these words.

WHICH IS HARDER THAN IT LOOKS

I no longer pretend to be a planner of activities and think that many of us are subject to T.M.A.

Too Many Activities

There is so much healing in prayers, stillness, meditation, and solitude.

I am still healing the part of me that fears not planning, or fears not having "enough activities!" My family loved doing activities, but we were also nappers, which saved my sensitive, creative spirit.

I often imagine the perfect social life and wonder who has one and what it consists of.

Yet I love my oddly shaped, strangely conceived social life, and I adore my private life.

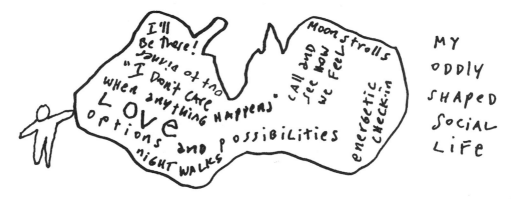

I'll be there!

"I don't care when anything happens"

LOVE options and possibilities

Sauvia et tno

night walks

Moon strolls

call and see how we feel

energetic check-in

MY ODDLY SHAPED SOCIAL LIFE

I've found that most people crave flexible plans and love to talk about planning differently. Many people also love cancelling and are thrilled to be encouraged to do it

I think that if you truly trust the flow of life and know that you are all ways surrounded by love, you don't care

Do you mind if we cancel our plans?

I'm thrilled!

Cancelling without consequences is exciting

<u>W h a t   H a p p e n s   W h e n</u>

What a relief

Join me in the flexible plan club, time stretcher/time shrinker, <u>Cancelling</u> <u>with no Consequences</u>, healing the tyranny of a beautiful day, and too many activities.

Let's decide to do something together and then happily cancel!

The clock

That makes you smile

Splendidly Human Moments

read this when you feel like everything BAD
happens to you

When I speak to gatherings of
people, I like to ask for stories of
what isn't working, what broke,
what has disturbed us, and more
importantly, stories of our splendid
and imperfect humanity. I also
like to call this "crabby time."

People share stories, and we are
woven together in our fragile,
funny, endearing human Bean-ness.

Recently, I went to my laundromat,
which is across the street. I was
dragging a lot of laundry in a big
black plastic garbage bag, which
was too heavy to lift. I heaved
this bag on top of a table and
noticed a terrible odor. I looked
down to see brown clumps and smears
of something on the table, the floor,

MY SHOES. I STARTED GAGGING. IT WAS
FRESH DOG POOP THAT I HAD DRAGGED IN
ON MY BAG FROM THE STREET AND IT
WAS ON EVERYTHING. OF COURSE, I WAS
TIRED AND IN A HURRY!

(IT WAS A SHITTY DAY.)

odiferous clumps

ANOTHER TIME, I WAS AT THE OFFICE OF
THE ORAL SURGEONS HAVING A ROOT CANAL,
AND THE HYGIENEST PUT A PLASTIC SHIELD
IN MY MOUTH. I BEGAN SWEATING AND
HYPERVENTILATING AND HAVING FLASHBACKS
OF CHILDHOOD INCEST. I FINALLY STOPPED
HER AND TORE THE PLASTIC OFF MY FACE.
AS SHE STARED AT ME WITH CONCERN, I
FINALLY MANAGED TO SAY THROUGH THE
TEARS,

"I WAS MOLESTED AS A CHILD, THE
PLASTIC MADE ME HAVE FLASHBACKS..."

SHE SMILED, SLAPPED ME ON THE
CHEST, AND PROCLAIMED,

"OH! DON'T YOU THINK ABOUT THAT
BAD THING!" WAIT. IT GETS EVEN WORSE.

At that moment, the lights went out, a siren went off, and over the intercom came the announcement that there had been an earthquake and we had to evacuate the building! I had to follow Ms. Sensitivity down the stairs. She froze and panicked, and I had to lead her out.

Was I kind? yes.

Here are two of my favorite crabby moments from people:

CRABBY MOMENTS ABOUND!

"I was driving on a winding mountain road and my dog threw up in my purse!"

"My 10-year-old son was singing very loudly in the car, over and over, the same obnoxious song. Finally I managed to say, 'Louder please, more, more!' He finally stopped."

I met a man in line at the supermarket who admitted being crabby. I congratulated him, and this led to the woman in front of me saying,

"I'm beyond crabby. It just took me 2 1/2 hours to get home from the airport because my boyfriend went to the wrong one! And he drives a junky car. In fact, it's so junky that he's outside in the car because it doesn't even lock!"

A dear woman named Trish shared this story:

"One of the shutters in our living room broke, and we went to Home Depot to get all new ones. The lady looked at the measurements and said cheerfully, 'Oh, I know exactly what you need!'

"The new shutters were unfinished, so I spent every night and weekend for two months sitting in my kitchen sanding and prepping and varnishing and missing the entire Olympics because I couldn't see the television. As I got to the last coat on the last section I noticed that the new shutters were the wrong size!"

(My) building has ancient plumbing and sometimes requires visits from a company called Drain Police. They come with hoses and machines and clear out the pipes.

My building was built in 1913

My property manager met them and supervised the job. I called in later to find out the results, and was told,

I couldn't resist drawing a tampon

"The guy says he found a mouse and came back to me holding it by the tail.
I looked closer to see that it was a tampon!
He was calling it a mouse as a joke."

It was my tampon, and two guys were holding it by the string. Discussing it! I was mortified. By the next day, I was able to share it as a splendidly human moment and laugh about it. HA!

160

I think we are starving to share
our crabby moments and splendidly
human stories. <u>We consistently think
that we are the</u> (only ones) and
then soften with relief when we
hear the stories of others.

Men sometimes worry that crabby
time will never end, so just ask to be
listened to with a time limit and
say that you will feel better at the end.
Don't forget to show that you do feel better!

Some people are crabby all the
time because they've never gotten
or given themselves permission
to be crabby in increments.

I used to teach art and adventures
to children and I would take
them to this store to visit
"the crabbiest man in the
world," which was what I
had named him.

He was crabby, but he
was also a wonderful artist

He thrived on his crabbiness and so did the kids. They opened up to me about what was really bothering them, what they actually worried and thought about.

When we can share our moments like these, we can usually laugh and feel the support of our community. We can also spend less time complaining or repeating negative patterns.

Person soars away from crabbiness after sharing it consciously

Find a splendidly human/crabby moment friend to trade stories with.

note: try setting a short time limit, ask for no solutions and report any positive outcome

What makes you crabby?

Who can you share stories of being splendidly human with?

Share crabby moments

HEALING WORK LIFE... YES, WE CAN

each Person Deserves work that nourishes and supports them.

The journey to find this work is different for all of us, and involves much self-exploration and "wrong" turns. Usually DisGuised Blessings!

Our work life operates as a series of lessons for our development as creative, fully engaged people. Sometimes the lesson entails leaving the work situation, adjusting the work situation, or re-creating the workplace.

I participated in many hundreds of jobs to find out what I didn't want to do or be, and to, in fact, find out more about who I actually was.

FASCINATING JOURNEY

I leaped HiGH and often

I took a number of leaps of faith to uncover my true work life, and risked everything to live the work life I had always envisioned.

risked everything

Working in this world is so full of
pitfalls, detours, tests, lessons, and
seductions. We must identify which work
steals the soul, and which supports the
soul, and spend our time in soul·supporting
work.

Try this: # SOUL Supporting

- inquire deeply into your work life
  and ask if it supports or steals your
  soul

  usually we know, it's just good to ask

- For soul·supporting work, whatever it
  may be, continue on and expand!

- For soul·stealing work, whatever it
  may be, make a plan to escape
  or detach, or stay on and be
  aware of the effects in your life

note: I have participated in many situations
       of both types, and there are many
       lessons to be learned from each one.

you can ride into a new work life at any time

       Healing our work lives can take many
       shapes. We can visualize and claim our
       true work life.

164

BOOKS/WHAT HEALS?

"NOW WITH GOD'S HELP I
SHALL BECOME MYSELF."

Søren Kierkegaard

Deep Play   By Diane Ackerman

The Highly Sensitive Person
By Elaine N. Aron Ph.D.

Emotional Intelligence
By Daniel Goleman

The Inner Child Workbook
By Cathryn Taylor

Wise Child: A Spiritual Guide to Nurturing
Your Child's Intuition
By Sonia Choquette

Forgiveness And Other Acts Of Love
By Stephanie Dowrick

www.iskip.com A Web Site Dedicated to Skipping!

"When your expectations Are not met,
you Are merely receiving A Correction.
You Are Being told that you Do not see
the Whole truth of A situation."
Paul Ferrini

Beginnings

The Distance Between inertia and Beginning
is so vast, that upon Contemplation, it
Appears too large to Cross.

inertia

Beginning

When we do Begin,
we make Discoveries.
We discover strengths
and Hopes, Dreams not
yet lived, Beloved
Hiding Places and
Parts of ourselves

We wish nobody could see.

it is much safer not to Begin

What if you Began A Dream and

it Didn't work

or, you were No Good At it, or
it Didn't satisfy you the way you Always
imagined?

What if you Began

and Quit?

My dad called me a quitter when I was 16 and faked my way into an archery instructor position at a summer camp (and then quit in desperation).

He echoed my worst fear about myself and became my "outer critic" and I feared starting anything for a very long time.

I've carefully chosen what I was best at, or was easiest for me, so nobody could call me a quitter again.

This meant that I missed out on a lot of experiences. Recently, on a cruise ship with my mom and brother, I deliberately tried three things I knew I wouldn't be very good at: swing dance lessons, karaoke, and chess.

My brother would want me to admit that I lasted about five minutes at chess

With each of these, I watched my frustration levels grow as I realized I couldn't be "the best." Yet I continued with each and enjoyed the experiences.

I began.

We can begin over and over, As many times As we want or need to. We can begin to change our Beliefs and the ways we categorize ourselves.

"Oh I've never been A good _____."

Begin Again!

I'm going to (Begin) to be:

A Person who easily tries many new things

A Person who is <u>sometimes</u> irritated

A Person who explores new tastes

A Person who travels lightly

A Person who <u>is</u>

I will continue to add new beginnings to this list!

Begin whatever it is over, if it doesn't feel nourishing to your soul and spirit. An 11-year-old Girl Just left me this message on my inspiration phone line:

"You remind me that my differences
from other people And ways I do
things Aren't weird, they're succulent!"

Begin it.

I WONDER...

WHAT CRUMBLES

WHere Grief leADS

How anGer Grows anD eVAPorATes

WHAT HAPPeneD to My BiG Deep
knee SCABS

WHY We Dont HAVe More eccentric
GATHeringS, teA PArties, anD SAlons

WHere We reAlly Go WHile sleepinG

WHY We Cant FinD FooD For
All the HUNGry

If our inside CHilDren HAVe FrienDs

WHAT THE introverts' restaurant
WOULD LOOK LiKE

How we can Feel Deeply loved More
of the Time

WHY Feeling separate still thrives

How to reach All of the Hurt, Hungry,
or lost Children

I wonder...

WHAT DO YOU wonder ?

Being A "reAL" Creative Person

My FrienD AndreA shAreD WiTh me
recenTly ThAT she DoesN'T Feel like A
"reAl" PAiNTer. SiNce I ADore AnD Am
iNspireD By Her PAiNTiNGs, I AskeD
Her To sAy WHY.

"BecAuse I PAiNT oN The GrounD
iNsTeAD oF UsiNG An eAsel, I Use AcrYlics,
noT Oils, I DiDN'T Go To ArT school,
I Don'T PAiNT OuT oF MY HeAD, I Use
imAGes, I holD The Brush WroNG. . ."

I sTopPeD Her To sAy ThAT I relATe
To AlmosT every one oF Her reAsons
AnD shAre similar FeArs, iNcLuDiNG This
one.

"I'M noT A 'reAl PAiNTer' BecAuse
I DoN'T Mix Colors NormAlly!" This
is iNsAne.

┌──┐
│ leT's All sTop CompAriNG ourselves   │
└──┘

To AnYone else
or AnY socieTAl sTAnDArDs ThAT We've
HeArD, WiTnesseD, or reAD AbouT.

We look At others And collect evidence
of How they're "really doing iT" And
Measure our own Attempts And Accomplishments
in this harsh lighting.

My Friend Adrienne told Me one Day,
"Well I Don't Feel like A very good
Mother. I got Home tired From work,
And Couldn't Get up to Fix Any Dinner
or turn off the tv. So I Finally got
cottage cheese And ritz crackers and
we laid on the Floor, eating and
watching whatever was on."

COTTAGE CHEESE

ritz crackers

doesn't this sound Delicious?

How could you Be A "real" parent and
not have these stories? Besides, the
Kid will Probably turn that into one
of Her Happiest Memories.

Tanya says, "I Don't think of Myself
As A 'real' writer Because I Don't
Write in My Journal every Day. Then
I realized that somehow, I still
have volumes of Finished Journals!"

Leigh wonders if she'll sing More
regularly. When I Ask Her if she has
Any Prospects, she says,

172

"OH YES! I'VE BEEN ASKED BY THIS POPULAR BAND TO SING ON SUNDAY NIGHTS WITH THEM." Please sing Leigh!

People often say to me,

"I'M NOT A 'REAL ARTIST.' I CAN'T EVEN draw a stick person!"

Then I say,

"Draw a toothpick, log, or yarn person! Draw y<u>our</u> <u>own</u> version!"

All kinds of stick figures

How can we grow creatively in all areas of our lives with all this comparing and judging, and fear of mistakes?

Our growth will suffer.

We might leap less high or limbo less often.

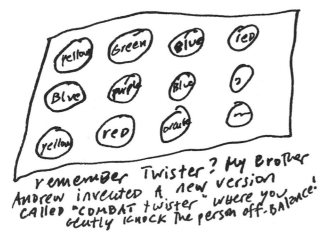

remember Twister? My brother Andrew invented a new version called "combat twister" where you gently knock the person off-balance!

We will slowly contract the experimentation of our very lives. This is what kills spirits.

This scarcity of experimenting can extend into all areas.

- Parenting is made of mistakes
  Please make more of them

- Aging is inevitable, restriction and contraction is a choice
  Please bounce against those walls

  Get more flexible as you age

- Extend more invitations without inviting rejection along

  Please come I'm o.k. if you don't

- Sing, write, paint, draw, create!
  Creativity loves mistakes!

AMAZING GRACE is extended to anyone who expands into something new.

Here is my list of what I'd love to try next:

- Traveling in a group   not in a small boat

- Lying down on an elephant and hugging it   My friend Jennifer hugged one named Eva

- Making something out of clay   Hopefully it will be very crooked

- Doing enough large paintings for a show   or having a smaller show!

- Wearing and loving a pair of lavender corduroy pants
- riding a horse again I get scared
- skiing I get scared
- loving in new ways I get really scared

Oh, there's so much to GOBBLE UP and dive into!

Let's magnify our heart's desires and manage to easily forget what has stopped us before. Let's chuckle at a dim memory of words that hurt us before and rush forward into the

N e w

into the

N o w

and be fully real people!

Being Creatively Seen in the World

We All Deserve to Be Creatively seen in this World.

Our Offerings Must Be Met By Thought·Full eyes and radiant Hearts.

It is good that So Many Are redefining this Word (Creativity) to include Us All.

We Are Creatively living Our lives and some of Us Feel Unseen and Certainly Unsung.

This is Sad
and Wrong

We idealize and idolize "Celebrities" in part to Avoid Meeting and expressing Our Own Creative selves.

We endow Others With the special Orb of Creativity and turn AWAY From

Our Own Creative yearnings and Murmurings.

We put other people in A "special orb of creativity" and leave ourselves out!

Sometimes the Murmurs Are really tiny

We look longingly at Bestseller lists or visit art galleries with no thought of seeing or displaying our own work.

We speak of having a "hobby" or "fooling around in a studio" and don't realize that this is creativity in action.

Creativity lives in gardens and children and walking, in bad jobs and crying at 4a.m.

creativity winds around everything we do

Creativity winds around everything we do.

How we perceive and share our lives can be done creatively or not.

If not, we suffer a dry life. If so, we live succulently.

Being seen creatively is entirely up to Y O U .

Jealousy, Competition, and Silences

In the underbrush lives my jealousy and competition. The other parts of me are bright sunlight and flowers, and then there is tangled underbrush I don't want anyone to see.

sunlight and flowers

Tangled underbrush

My jealousy springs from a primitive fear that there isn't enough or that I am not enough.

I measure and compare myself to others and try to see if their success seems more than mine. Meanwhile, others are doing this to me!

More! More!

There is a pact of (silence) about this, a general acknowledgment of the unpleasantness of jealousy and competition.

This is also the work of an inner critic gone awry. This inner critic guards the gates, promotes success and accomplishment, and pushes us even when it isn't healthy.

It is also the work of the ego, which stands for

Edging God Out

To compete and feel less than if we perceive loss is evidence of the shadowy, lost parts of ourselves.

The more we deny these shadows or resist the tangled underbrush, the more ominous the dark feelings can become.

It is a relief to express it somehow: To the person, your journal, or on a "stomping angry mud walk" as my friend Vanessa does.

The good for one is truly the good for all, and the separation we feel at another's good is really just separation from spirit and from divine goodness.

We GAVE away a lot...

let's multiply and MAGNIFY

Goodness

It can be so difficult to be authentically glad for someone else when you feel that it takes something away from you. We need to probe those illusions and discover our wounded and tangled places that prevent us from offering our own goodness to this world.

We must not be silent and lost in our own underbrush.

person tries to crawl out of the underbrush

We can shine a light there too and tenderly admit where we feel we are lacking, or lost, or less than.

shine a light there too...

Every single person has felt this no matter what level of success he or she has achieved. This achieved success can contribute to a cover-up of the core of the matter.

We can race to accomplish, to cover up tiny broken cracks or places we judge too ugly to be seen.

UGLY stuff

We rush to cover up, to put a lid on our lacking places... it doesn't work

The true achievement comes in our admissions of our weaknesses, jealousies, vulnerabilities, and places within still seeking healing.

BOOKS / Creative Healings

"The new era is the
era of spiritual creativity."
Henry Miller

The Right to Write   By Julia Cameron

Never Good Enough
                By Monica Ramirez Basco

Spilling Open   By Sabrina Ward Harrison

Still Mostly True
or Any Other Book By Brian Andreas
                www.storypeople.com

Mango Elephants in the Sun
                By Susana Herrera

Writing Past Dark   By Bonnie Friedman

Life, Paint And Passion   By Michell Cassou
                And Stewart Cubley

The Art Spirit   By Robert Henri

Transitions   By Julia Cameron

"All Great Art is A visual Form
of Prayer."   Sister Wendy

"To live A Creative life, We Must
lose our Fear of Being Wrong."
                Joseph Chilton Pearce

Your Own Healing Book

This book is meant to support you in your healing. I also encourage you to begin your own healing book.

1. Get a blank book that you love.

2. Collect pens and markers and crayons, or pencils!

3. Follow my chapter headings and write your own stories, or make up your own chapter headings.

4. Expand and add to your own healing book as your life shifts and changes.

The documentation and expression of healing is very important for our culture and for our own lives as we live them. To express and explain and experience our own healing process can enable us to be more fully present in it, or to assist others.

Let others share in your healing stories, and be affected by theirs.

Healing Circles

We sit in circles to connect and bond with other humans. Our stories reach WAY beyond ourselves when shared.

I shared my template for succulent wild woman groups in previous books. This book calls for the formation of healing circles.

It can be as simple as sitting in a circle as each person shares a story of something she or he has healed, or is healing. You can also form specific circles for certain kinds of healing.

All of us are engaged and involved with healing our own lives. People love to share healing stories, and often need an initiator or leader to begin an informal or formal process.

Think of one other person who may be interested. Call, e-mail, or write her or him. Form a circle with two, and then perhaps add to it.

circular motion

Acceptance of Healing

As I write these words, I am recovering from a fall and from poison oak. My friend Debra said, "Did you need any <u>more</u> material for your healing book?" I hadn't thought so...

It is curious how we are sometimes led to the experiences that we need for spiritual, physical, or emotional growth. I have begun to realize that healing is an opportunity presented all the time, and that we can choose our responses to it.

Acceptance of healing is a very specific choice. It involves surrender and release of denial and defenses. I didn't want to accept that I fell off a hiking trail while not paying attention, and then I didn't accept the actuality of my injuries. I tried to hurry past the healing lessons.

HEALING LESSONS

Trying to dash past the healing lessons

I returned to my life and work, dragging my hurt leg and swallowing lots of Aspirin. I felt irritated and affronted by these injuries, impatient at the recovery time.

Certainly I had nothing to learn about Acceptance, did I?

I find that my lessons repeat or magnify themselves if I am trying to hide from or ignore their message. So, a week later, poison oak bloomed.

From a few dots

I had to cancel things, admit vulnerabilities, ask for help!

Was this part of my Acceptance lesson?

to OOZING Desperate Welts of Agony

and this is an understatement!

As I cried and scratched and tried not to scratch and applied every kind of balm, tincture, homeopathic remedy, and herb...

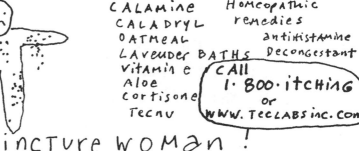

Calamine
Caladryl
Oatmeal
Lavender Baths
Vitamin E
Aloe
Cortisone
Tecnu

Homeopathic remedies
antihistamine
Decongestant

Call
1·800·itching
or
www.teclabsinc.com

I became... Tincture Woman!

I HAD TO STOP EXERCISING, WORKING,
DOING. ALL THINGS I STILL DERIVE
THE ILLUSION OF IDENTITY FROM.

We Are not
The T★ings
We Do

   FINALLY I (CRAWLED) TOWARD ACCEPTANCE
OF THE HEALING BY REALIZING THAT I AM
NOW FULLY ENGAGED IN THE LESSONS PRESENTED.
I AM NO LONGER TURNING AWAY OR TRYING TO
r   u   s   H   P   a   s   T

   IT IS SO TEMPTING TO JUST WANT
THINGS TO BE OVER, TO GET
PAST IT, TO PUT IT BEHIND YOU.

   MY FRIEND PATRICIA CALLED IT
MY "WAKE-UP FALL." IT ALSO INVOLVED
A BRUSH WITH POTENTIALLY FAR MORE
SERIOUS CONSEQUENCES.

   I WAS HANGING UPSIDE DOWN AND
BACKWARD ON THE EDGE OF A VERY
STEEP DROP-OFF, IN A ROW OF BUSHES
THAT TURNED OUT TO BE LAVENDER,

I WAS SAVED
BY lAVENDER!

MiXeD WiTH PoiSoN OAK.

My 11-year-old niece, Emily, helped to
pull me out. We hiked on, and I was
oblivious to the extent of my injuries.

That night, I cried in my bed
at the idea of tumbling down that
cliff, and was reminded once
again that _every_ _moment_ is our
exquisite gift.

THE ECSTATIC NOW!

THIS
iS
WHAT
WE HAVE

Healing is our curriculum and
our classroom, whether we want to be
in school or not.

I choose to accept the lessons.

Here Are Four Areas of Healing Study I Highly recommend and How They Function in My life:

1. Procrastination:

This Works Well As A sabotaging technique. It Also serves Well to enable Avoidance. There Are tempting Gifts Within it, the largest Being: suffocation Of true Potential. I have Been studying and experiencing the effects Of Procrastination For About 20 years. I've Described Myself As A "recovering Procrastinator." I've learned Copious Amounts About Completion By studying Procrastination.

readings: <u>Procrastination</u>: <u>Why You Do It</u>, <u>What to Do About It</u>
By Lenora Yuen Ph.D. And Jane Burka Ph.D.
<u>The Tomorrow Trap</u> By Karen Peterson Ph.D.

2. Inner Critic Work:

You Can learn to Dialogue With Critical inner voices, and turn them into Allies. I've Been Dabbling With and Delving into this Work For About 10 years. I Consider it to Be one Of the Most Potent And Deep Forms Of self-healing. I Also Find it extraordinarily Difficult and Scary. There Are Many Different Kinds Of voices and I Keep Uncovering new Areas For healing.

readings: Any Books or tapes By Hal and Sidra Stone

info: Hal And Sidra Stone, Ph.D
Delos Inc.
P.O. Box 604
Albion, CA 94510-0604
707.937.2424   www.delos-inc.com

3. Inner Child: I like to call it "inside child"

　　We all have a cast of characters inside that represent the child parts of us at various ages and stages of development. I've been studying this for about 15 years, and just in the last two years have truly been reparenting those inner children and learning how to be a full adult. It is truly liberating and life altering to be doing this work, and has changed my entire life/living experience. I intensely recommend this work to anyone who is drawn to it.

readings:　The Inner Child Workbook by Cathryn Taylor
　　　　　every single book by Cheri Huber

4. Creative Evolution:

　　I've been an active artist/creative person for my entire life, and continue to discover new terrain, paths, and places to explore. My creative life serves me, saves me, and inspires me daily. I have been described as a "creative nut." This is good.

　　I have, and have had, many teachers and mentors on my creative path.

　　I wish the same for you.

readings:　The Artist's Way by Julia Cameron
　　　　　Vein of Gold by Julia Cameron
　　　　　In My Own Way by Alan Watts
　　　　　Jenny Read by Jenny Read
　　　　　Spilling Open by Sabrina Ward Harrison
　　　　　Orbiting the Giant Hairball by Gordon MacKenzie

Permission to Heal and Feel Pure Support

May you be FLOODED with Permission to Heal. May this permission infuse everything that you do and are.

Ask yourself these questions:

(AM I making my most Alive Choices?)

note: these can feel tingly, scary, solid, bursting with life

(AM I signing up for Change?)

note: rather than passively responding to change, Actively embracing it

(AM I intimately engaged in my own life?)

note: this can feel messy, out of control, and very dark at times

(AM I Creatively Fulfilled?)

note: Do you express, create, make something new each day? Why or why not?

(AM I surrounded by/Creating A healing support system?)

note: We need lots of hugs and safe containers for all of our feelings. Is this an area of expansion or Contraction for you?

SAFe containers

Your Answers to these Questions reveal Areas of Fulfillment and of lack.

Remember: (love is expansion GROWING)
Fear is Contraction

SHrinKing

What expands you, feeds you, fills you?

Begin to tease out threads from knots that may have developed years ago from woundings and just-not-knowings.

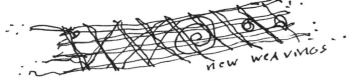

The thread will lead you somewhere

We are beings of light, and whatever obscures that light can be tenderly and carefully examined. The results of these examinations can be woven into our lives in new ways.

new weavings

This is not about eradicating mistakes, bad feelings, or negativity, or living in some la-la-land of positivity. It is <u>most</u> <u>certainly</u> <u>not</u> about turning away from the dark.

The dark holds our roots and shoots, and bulbs of growth

It is about using pain as a healer and teacher, receiving the lessons and acting from wise places with support and guidance.

Please search for and use your support systems to heal.

Any healing you do affects us all.

BOOKS/HEALING WAYS of BEING

"I DREAMT... /THAT I HAD A BEEHIVE/
HERE INSIDE MY HEART./AND THE GOLDEN
BEES/WERE MAKING WHITE COMBS/
AND SWEET HONEY/FROM ALL MY OLD
FAILURES."

ANTONIO MACHADO
(TRANSLATED BY ROBERT BLY)

A Year to Live BY STEPHEN LEVINE

One Day My Soul Just Opened Up BY IYANLA VANZANT

I Was My Mother's Bridesmaid
BY ERICA CARLISLE AND VANESSA CARLISLE

The Rule Of Two BY ANN WOODIN AND ANDREW RUSH
OBSERVATIONS ON
CLOSE RELATIONSHIP   CALL 520.896.2446 OR WRITE ORACLE PRESS
P.O. BOX 160 ORACLE, AZ 85623

MUSIC: THE VELVET JANES WEB SITE: WWW.VELVETJANES.COM.AU
BAABA MAAL/NOMAD SOUL

MAGAZINE: THE SUN   WWW.THESUNMAGAZINE.ORG
888.732.6736
THE SUN P.O. BOX 3000
DENVILLE, NJ 07834
A NOURISHING AND DEMANDING MAGAZINE

"LOVE MANY. TRUST A FEW.
LEARN TO PADDLE YOUR OWN CANOE."
AUTHOR UNKNOWN

TUB OF LOVE

LiFe is A TuB of Love

immerse Your seLF

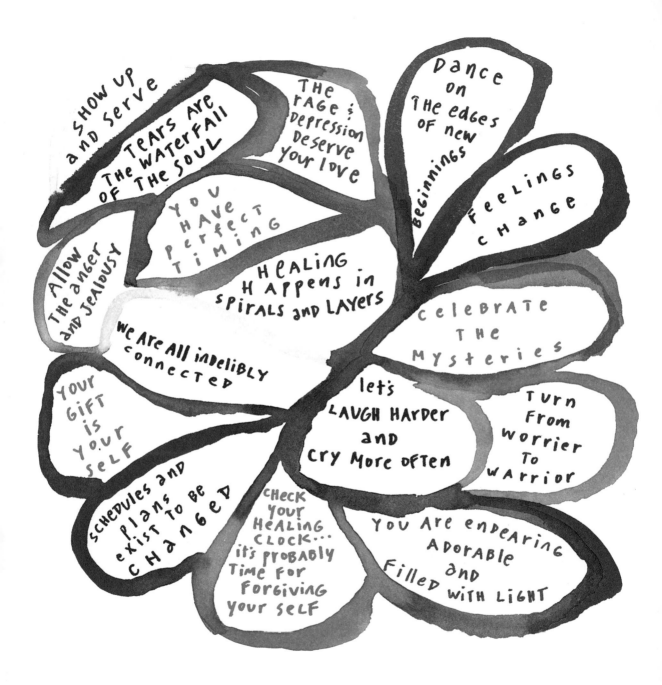

OH BEAUTY YOUR angel Lives inside OF YOU

love. SARK

The Transformative

TO REACH US AT CAMP SARK:

CAMP SARK is a company that designs and creates products for creative living. Our mission is to spread the spirit of SARK ÷ a philosophy that says we are each creatively gifted and need to share those gifts.

WWW. CAMPSARK. COM
COOL creative web site

or call: 415. 397. 7275 (SARK) for general information

e mail: CAMPSARK@BEST.COM   24 Hours

write: P.O. BOX 330039 San Francisco CA 94133

Subscribe to SARK's MAGIC MUSE letter! See last page of this book

---

LOOK for SARK's inspired Gift collection in stores near you   CARDS, CALENDARS, POSTERS, STATIONERY, BLANKETS, WATCHES, and, more! For more information on how to purchase SARK Gift items, call CAMP SARK at 415. 397. SARK (7275) 24 Hours or visit our website at WWW. CAMPSARK.COM

The inspiration line is a place to be how you actually are. Tears are welcome. So is silence.
   SARK speaks for 3-5 minutes. She quotes people, sometimes she sings. Join the family of people that call from all over the world

SARK's inspiration Line 24 Hours
415
546
3742
(epic)

WORLD of SARK

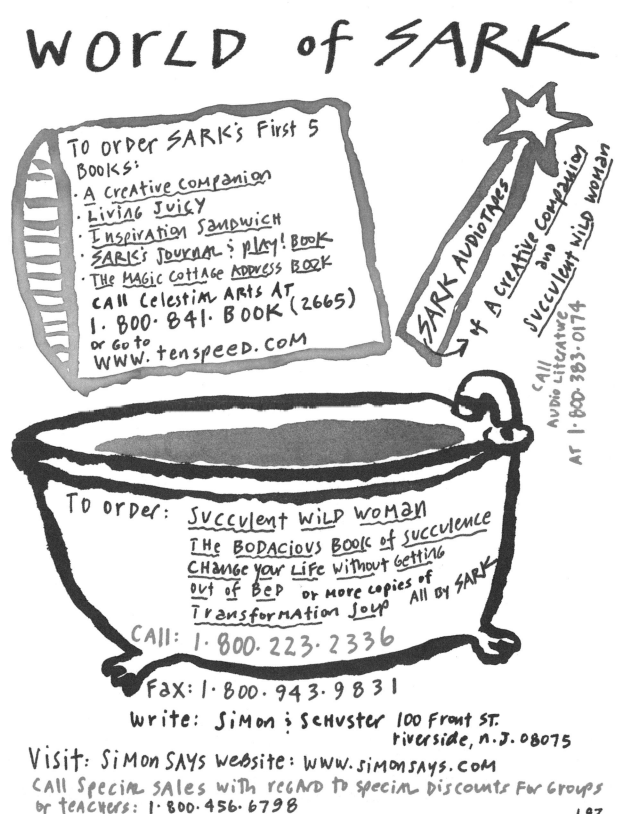

TO order SARK's First 5
Books:
- A creative companion
- Living Juicy
- Inspiration Sandwich
- SARK's Journal & play! Book
- The magic cottage Address Book

CAll Celestial Arts AT
1·800·841·BOOK (2665)
or Go to
WWW. tenspeed. com

SARK AUDIOTAPES
of A creative companion
and
succulent wild woman
CAll
Audio Literature
AT 1·800·383·0174

TO order: Succulent wild woman
The BODACiOUS BOOK of Succulence
change your life without Getting
out of Bed or more copies of
Transformation Soup All By SARK

CAll: 1·800·223·2336

Fax: 1·800·943·9831

Write: Simon & Schuster 100 Front St.
riverside, n.J. 08075

Visit: Simon SAYS website: www. simonsays. com

CAll Special sales with regard to special discounts for Groups
or teachers: 1·800·456·6798

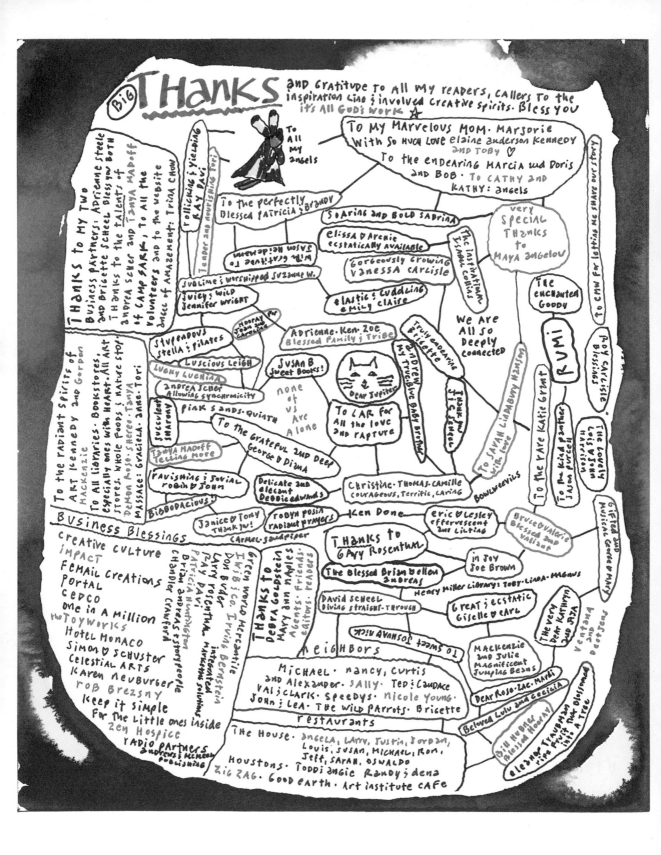

SARK'S MAGIC Museletter

YOU Are A Gift Th

There is A MAGIC CottAGE inside eAch of us

DeAr Angel FAces,

[handwritten letter text, actual size 11x24 inches]

For Love And HeALing,

SARK

ACTUAL Size 11x24 inches

Oh Succulent HeALing Ones,

This is your Personal invitation to the Magic Museletter. This is An AmAzing WAY to Keep you And I connected in BetWeen HeALing naps And Bursts of Creativity. The Magic Museletter WAS Born in 1996 And now Goes out to many thousands of People Around the World. I Am continually inspired By the voices that AppeAr Within the PAges of this fAbulous publication.

A subscription to the Magic Museletter includes A GIANT, Full Color letter From me, Advance peeks into my new books, the latest Camp SARK Adventures, Full color Artwork And Chances for you to submit your own Artwork And Writing!

Until the next Museletter, I send you splendidly imperfect HeALing, the Gift of surrender And Absolute Love.

Very DeArly, SARK

Here's WhAt you can look ForWArd to in the Museletter:

☆ Each issue includes a 17" x 24" Inspirational letter from SARK that focuses on different themes. Some back issues themes have included: Healing, Friendship, Succulence, and Comfort.

☁ Inner Views–Wild Imaginings with highly creative people (which we all are!).

◎ Subscriber's Contribute–An opportunity for your art and writing to be published in the Museletter!

☆ SARK's latest calendar & book gathering dates.

◎ Ripe News from Camp and more!

To order back issues of the Museletter, send check or money order for $4.50 per issue (includes shipping and handling) or $6.50 per issue for all foreign orders (US funds only please!) to Camp SARK, Attn: ML Back issues, PO Box 330039, SF, CA 94133. For credit card orders, please fill out information on subscription card on next page.
Special Offer! You may order any eight back issues of the Museletter for $30.00, a savings of $6.00. All Foreign orders, $45.00 for eight back issues, a savings of $7.00.

www.campsark.com

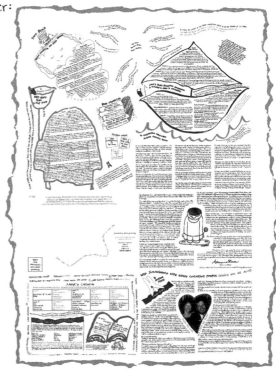

ACTUAL Size 17x24 inches

Yes!

Please sign me up to receive a two-year, eight-issue subscription of **SARK's Magic Museletter.**
Please send this card and payment to:

Camp SARK

Attn: Museletter, PO Box 330039,
San Francisco, CA 94133

Rates are as follows: Regular–$23, "**Star** achie**vi**ng Artist"–$19.50, Child 12 & Under $19.50, All Foreign Orders–$28 *(payable in U.S. funds only)* Checks, credit cards and money orders accepted. Checks made payable to Camp SARK.

Send a Friend a Gift!

There will be so much inspiration and information in **SARK's Magic Museletter,** you'll want to share it with your friends and family. The Museletter is a unique gift to give and to receive. It will provide two years' worth of creativity and fun at a great price! Please choose a rate for your gift subscription and send it along with your payment to the above address. A gift card will be sent to the recipient to announce their new subscription.

Please allow 6-8 weeks for delivery of your first issue.

SARK'S Magic Museletter
Subscriber Information

1

Name	Phone #	E-mail

Address	City	State	Zip (+4 digits)

Rates:*(circle one)* Regular–$23   "Starving Artist" or Child 12 & Under–$19.50   All Foreign Orders–$28 *(U.S. funds only)*

2

Name	Phone #	E-mail

Address	City	State	Zip (+4 digits)

Rates:*(circle one)* Regular–$23   "Starving Artist" or Child 12 & Under–$19.50   All Foreign Orders–$28 *(U.S. funds only)*

Credit Card # (MC/Visa only)	Signature of Cardholder

Expiration Date	Billing address Zip code (if different from above)

Order 1 is a Gift Subscription* from: _____

Order 2 is a Gift Subscription* from: _____

TS

Please allow 6-8 weeks for delivery of your first issue.
***A gift card will be mailed to recipient.**